Issues in Contemporary Theology
Series Editor: I. Howard Marshall

The Origins of New Testament Christology
I. Howard Marshall

The Search for Salvation
David F. Wells

Christian Hope and the Future
Stephen H. Travis

Theology Encounters Revolution
J. Andrew Kirk

Christian Hope & the Future

Stephen H. Travis

InterVarsity Press
Downers Grove
Illinois 60515

© *Stephen H. Travis 1980*

Printed in America by InterVarsity Press, Downers Grove, Illinois, with permission from Universities and Colleges Christian Fellowship, Leicester, England.

InterVarsity Press is the book-publishing division of Inter-Varsity Christian Fellowship, a student movement active on campus at hundreds of universities, colleges and schools of nursing. For information about local and regional activities, write IVCF, 233 Langdon St., Madison, WI 53703.

Distributed in Canada through InterVarsity Press, 1875 Leslie St., Unit 10, Don Mills, Ontario M3B 2M5, Canada.

Unless otherwise stated, quotations from the Bible are from the Revised Standard Version, copyrighted 1946, 1952, © *1971, 1973, by the Division of Christian Education, National Council of the Churches of Christ in the USA, and used by permission.*

ISBN 0-87784-463-1
Library of Congress Catalog Card Number: 80-7471

Printed in the United States of America

17	16	15	14	13	12	11	10	9	8	7	6	5	4	3	2	1
94	93	92	91	90	89	88	87	86	85	84	83	82	81	80		

Preface

Christianity without hope is an impossibility. But hope for what? Hopes expressed in the New Testament raise difficult questions both for the reader seeking to understand what the authors meant and for the interpreter attempting to convey what those hopes can mean for us today. I have tried in this book to analyse significant contributions to the modern debate about these questions, to draw attention to some of the key issues, and to indicate some conclusions of my own.

Perhaps the title requires a word of explanation. Since the emergence of the 'theology of hope' associated with theologians like Jürgen Moltmann, it has become common to link terms such as 'hope' and 'future' almost exclusively with man's future *in this world*. I do not wish for a moment to minimize the importance of that theme – which would require a book in itself. But maybe the excitement surrounding this recent theological development has led in some circles to a neglect of Christian teaching on God's *ultimate* purposes for mankind. So I offer the following chapters, fully aware that their treatment of Christian hope is not comprehensive, but convinced that their themes are crucial both for biblical scholarship and for Christian believing.

I am grateful to Professor Howard Marshall, Dr Richard Bauckham and Dr David Cook for their encouragement, criticisms and suggestions; and to many students, colleagues and friends who have raised the questions which I have tried to grapple with in this book.

Abbreviations

ExpT	*Expository Times*
JBL	*Journal of Biblical Literature*
JTC	*Journal for Theology and the Church*
JTS	*Journal of Theological Studies*
NBD	*The New Bible Dictionary* (1962)
NTS	*New Testament Studies*
SJT	*Scottish Journal of Theology*
TDNT	*Theological Dictionary of the New Testament* (ET, 1964–76)
TynB	*Tyndale Bulletin*
ZRG	*Zeitschrift für Religions- und Geistesgeschichte*

Chapter One

The problem of eschatology

For many millennia human beings have thought about the future. Of all creatures, man, it appears, is the only one who knows he is going to die. The evidence of burial rituals from twenty thousand years ago, and of literature in more recent times indicates man's concern with death and his almost universal sense of a life (or lives) beyond death.[1] Also widespread has been man's sense of the imperfection of his present lot, which has impelled him to seek for a better future within this world. This has been expressed, for example, in the Greek and Roman longing for the return of a golden age, in Plato's plan for an ideal republic, in Marxism's expectation of the classless society. Within Judaism the twin hope of a life beyond death for the individual and for society emerged towards the end of the Old Testament period. Its distinctive form was motivated primarily by a sense of God's justice (which required that wrongs not righted during the present life of the individual or during the present historical era should be righted after death or in a future era); and by a sense of God's love, which could not allow fellowship between God and man to be cut short by death.[2] These hopes became sharply focused through the teaching and work of Jesus of Nazareth. Hence there arose 'Christian eschatology', which is the subject of this book.

There are many reasons for the current interest in eschatology inside and outside scholarly circles. It has been said, for example, that when a society senses that it is at the end of an era it contemplates death. Interestingly, N. Q. Hamilton, writing in 1960, commented that eschatology tends to be important to those who personally and socially have reached the end of worldly order and security, and

[1] See the two symposia by A. Toynbee and others, *Man's Concern with Death* (London, 1968), and *Life After Death* (London, 1976).
[2] See the summary in P. Badham, *Christian Beliefs about Life after Death* (London, 1976), pp. 3–17.

cited the German-speaking churches in the 1940s as an example. Americans, he said, have less sympathy for 'beyonds' because circumstances have never forced such thoughts upon them, and so they disparage eschatology.[3] But since he wrote, the popular imagination has been turned to 'eschatology' by events such as the assassination of President Kennedy, the impact of the Vietnam war, the Watergate affair and the oil crisis. The spread of environmental pollution, the threat of nuclear radiation, and the rapid depletion of the earth's non-renewable resources raise enormous question marks against our civilization's ability to survive.

At the same time 'futurology' has developed. This is the business of estimating what a society will be like in, say, twenty-five or fifty years' time by extrapolating from current social, political, technological and economic trends.[4] The impression that one's future is being controlled by statisticians and technocrats can create anxiety. And it leads people to ask whether society as predicted by this method is the kind of society they want. So, once again, thoughts are turned towards the future.

Also, the secular 'eschatologies' of Marxism, Fascism and optimistic humanism have demonstrated that even if a religiously-based eschatology is abandoned, men have a knack of finding some other object of hope. And that suggests that man is a creature of hope who cannot for long suppress his inbuilt desire for 'a better world'.[5]

At the level of biblical scholarship the nineteenth century saw development of historico-critical methods and growing awareness of the Jewish background of Jesus. This led to a revolution in understanding of Jesus' message about the kingdom of God, which will be sketched below. Its impact on biblical and theological scholarship has continued without subsiding.

[3] 'The Last Things in the Last Decade', *Interpretation* 14, 1960, pp. 131f.
[4] See, for example, the books by Herman Kahn, *The Year 2000* (New York, 1967); *Things to Come* (New York, 1972); *The Next 200 Years* (New York, 1976). There is a brief discussion of such approaches in Harvey Cox, *On Not Leaving It to the Snake* (London, 1968), pp. 31ff. (though I do not entirely agree with his analysis there of the difference between 'prophetic' and 'apocalyptic' perspectives).
[5] For a splendid evaluation of idealism and utopianism see the appendix to H. Thielicke, *The Evangelical Faith*, 1 (ET, Grand Rapids, 1974), pp. 386–403.

Difficulties of eschatology

It is time we paused to define what we are talking about. For 'eschatology' is a 'slippery word': its meaning has been changed so much that it is in danger of being meaningless.[6] According to J. Carmignac, the term 'eschatology' was first used in 1804 with reference to all that Jesus still has to do as Lord and Judge of men, including everything which pertains to the destiny of man from his death onwards.[7] Etymologically the term should mean 'the doctrine or science of the last things', and should refer to such things as the parousia (this technical term for the 'second coming' of Christ will sometimes be used in this book, especially in chapter 5), the resurrection of the dead, heaven and hell. Carmignac pleads that the word be used only in this sense, and this is the sense it will normally have in this book.

But we should be alert to the fact that the term has often been overlaid with other meanings. Albert Schweitzer, for example, meant by it not simply 'the doctrine of the last things' but 'the belief that the last things *are near*.[8] Many more recent writers have used the adjective 'eschatological' in much the same way as we use the word 'ultimate': the sense of 'last' in time has been superseded by the sense of 'ultimate' or 'final' in significance. This is the case, for example, with Bultmann and with the advocates of various versions of 'realized eschatology'. Marshall surveys nine distinct meanings of 'eschatology' and 'eschatological', and his list is not exhaustive. Jürgen Moltmann's *Theology of Hope*, for instance, frequently uses these words, but it is not a book about the traditional 'last things'.

Even if a definition is agreed, the study of eschatology has its peculiar problems. It is concerned with things which have not yet happened, and with 'things' (such as life after death) which are a matter of faith rather than empirical proof. Objectivity in study is therefore even more difficult than with, say, christology. It is not very surprising that – as one adaptation of Matthew 11:12 has it – 'Everyone forces the kingdom of God violently into his own theological tradition.'[9]

[6] I. H. Marshall, 'Slippery Words: 1. Eschatology', in *ExpT* 89, 1977-8, pp. 264–269.
[7] J. Carmignac, 'Les dangers de l'eschatologie', *NTS* 17, 1970–71, pp. 365–390.
[8] See I. H. Marshall, *ExpT* 89, p. 265.
[9] R. H. Hiers, 'Eschatology and Methodology', *JBL* 85, 1966, p. 183.

Moreover, because eschatology deals with what 'has never entered the heart of man', it raises in acute form the problem of language. Some kind of picture-language seems inevitable when we are speaking about realities which lie both temporally and spatially beyond our present experience. What is the relationship between that language and those realities (assuming, of course, that they *are* real)? Were the biblical writers able to distinguish between 'literal' and 'pictorial' or 'mythical' language, or did they use such language without reflecting on its precise relationship to reality? And – whatever may have been the case with them – how are we, with our 'modern world-view', to handle the Bible's language about the parousia, about judgment, heaven and hell?

Despite such difficulties, there is no escaping the crucial importance of eschatology for Christian life and faith. It is at, or very close to, the heart of the New Testament message. A coherent eschatology is required – and here I am asserting what will be considered more carefully later – if a believer in God is to make sense of the ambiguities of the world. For Wolfhart Pannenberg comments that 'in some sense atheism has a point in arguing that the world ought to be different if there were a God who cares for man and even for every individual. . . . Only the full manifestation of God's kingdom in the future . . . can finally decide about the reality of God.'[10] Whether or not we agree with Pannenberg's general theological position, he is surely right to stress the importance of eschatology for theodicy. But it is not only the ambiguities and injustices of the world which require an eschatology. The Christian experience of God as one who holds persons to be of supreme value would be called into question if that experience were to be terminated by death or by whatever end this universe may undergo.

Developments in eschatology

It is quite arbitrary to begin a sketch of developments in theology (or in anything else) at one date rather than another. But a brief reference to some earlier treatments of issues discussed in this book will help us to gain perspective.

---

[10] 'Can Christianity do without an Eschatology?' in G. B. Caird *et al.*, *The Christian Hope* (London, 1970), p. 31.

Christian eschatology at its outset inherited a tension between individual eschatology ('what happens to me when I die?') and the corporate eschatology of a resurrection when the 'Son of man' comes at the end of the present age. For the tension was already there in Judaism.[11] Rarely have the two understandings been happily harmonized, and the attention of Christian thinkers has almost invariably been concentrated on one or other strand of hope rather than on both. Even today there are many books on either topic separately, but very few that treat both together.[12] Thus the two 'branches' of eschatology developed fairly independently.

Questions about the individual's death, his judgment, heaven and hell were much debated in the nineteenth century, in Britain, in America and on the Continent. J. Carmignac refers to a book published in America in 1864 which listed 4,894 items under the heading, 'Literature of the Doctrine of a Future Life: Or, a Catalogue of Works relating to the Nature, Origin and Destiny of the Soul'.[13]

Among many liberal thinkers influenced by the Enlightenment and by German Idealism the idea of immortality (rather than a more explicitly Christian doctrine of eternal life) seemed congenial enough. But it was based on metaphysical and ethical principles rather than on the word or work of Christ. In Friedrich Schleiermacher there is a constant tension between the philosopher and the theologian: he attempted to base his belief in the survival of personality on the word of Christ alone, having had serious doubts about it on other grounds.[14] Such doubts became more widespread in an age of growing confidence in natural science, technology and socialism – all of which encouraged preoccupation with the present world. But there was no more obvious casualty of these trends than the doctrine of hell: W. E. Gladstone commented at the end of the nineteenth century that this doctrine had been 'relegated . . . to the far-off corners of the Christian mind . . . there to sleep in deep shadow as

---

[11] See below, pp. 95ff.

[12] Among books which do offer a comprehensive treatment may be mentioned P. Althaus, *Die letzten Dinge* (Gütersloh, 1922, [7]1957); E. Brunner, *The Christian Doctrine of the Church, Faith and the Consummation: Dogmatics*, 3 (ET, London, 1962); H. Schwarz, *On the Way to the Future* (Minneapolis, 1972); and more briefly, J. Macquarrie, *Christian Hope* (Oxford, 1978).

[13] *NTS*, 1970–1, p. 365, n. 2.

[14] See *The Christian Faith* (ET, Edinburgh, 1928), pp. 698–713 (the German original appeared in 1821–2).

a thing needless in our enlightened and progressive age.'[15]

Within ecclesiastical circles, the new spirit of enquiry made it more possible than previously to air doubts and suggest alternative theories of human destiny. Hence the nineteenth century witnessed some notable controversies, carefully and colourfully described by Geoffrey Rowell in *Hell and the Victorians*. In 1853 F. D. Maurice was dismissed from his professorship at King's College, London, for denying eternal punishment and refusing to believe that death brought an end to hope. Similar views were advocated by F. W. Farrer in *Eternal Hope* (1878). Neither was a universalist, though they were widely believed to be such. The ensuing spate of tracts, such as E. B. Pusey's *What is of Faith as to Everlasting Punishment?* (1880), failed to stop the spread of the belief that all men will ultimately find salvation. Bishop Colenso of Natal (later famous for his questioning the historicity of the Pentateuch) had in his *Village Sermons* (1853) argued for a form of universalism, based on the 'universalist passages' in Paul's epistles and on the widespread belief in a remedial process after death. His missionary experience, which led him to believe that the doctrine of eternal punishment was a hindrance rather than a spur to missionary endeavour, lay behind his teaching. A full-blown universalist doctrine was advocated by Andrew Jukes in *The Second Death and the Restitution of All Things* (1867) and by Samuel Cox in *Salvator Mundi* (1877).[16] Over the last hundred years this doctrine has continued to gain support. Although it has been expressed in more subtle forms, and with the support of a more informed, more sophisticated and sometimes more negative approach to the Bible, it has not been based on any arguments substantially different from those already used in the nineteenth century.[17]

That century also witnessed the powerful advocacy of 'conditional immortality' as an alternative to eternal torment. In essence, this

---

[15] *Studies Subsidiary to the Works of Bishop Butler* (1896), p. 206; quoted in G. Rowell, *Hell and the Victorians* (Oxford, 1974), p. 212.

[16] G. Rowell, *ibid.*, pp. 129–133. Universalism was also quite prevalent in other European countries: see G. Müller, 'Die Idee einer Apokatastasis ton panton in der europäischen Theologie von Schleiermacher bis Barth', *ZRG* 16, 1964, pp. 1–22.

[17] R. J. Bauckham has shown clearly how new ways of handling the Bible have played their part in the transition from Victorian to more modern forms of universalism in 'Universalism: a Historical Survey', *Themelios* 4.2, January 1979, p. 52.

doctrine is that God created man mortal but with a capacity for immortality; this immortality is bestowed on those who have faith in Christ, whilst those who do not have faith are annihilated, either at death or after a period of just punishment. It thus starts from a different premise from that of the immortality of the soul which was generally assumed both by believers in eternal torment and by universalists. One of the most famous exponents of the doctrine was the Congregationalist Ernest White, whose main work *Life in Christ* appeared in 1845. Like Colenso, he was moved by the state of the heathen and their ignorance of Christ, questioned the grounding of missionary work in the doctrine of eternal punishment, and proposed conditionalism as a more just alternative. In America C. F. Hudson wrote a careful systematic defence of the theory, particularly in relation to theodicy (*Debt and Grace as related to the Doctrine of a Future Life*, [2]1858). The leading continental conditionalist was the Swiss Emmanuel Pétavel-Olliff, whose main book (1891) appeared in English translation as *The Problem of Immortality* (1892). He, like many other nineteenth-century conditionalists, put more weight on philosophical than on exegetical arguments. Others, too, made much of man's affinity with animals, as popularized by Darwinism, in their argument that man is not naturally immortal. In the twentieth century support for conditionalism has owed more to developments in the understanding of biblical anthropology and to the biblical emphasis on 'resurrection' as opposed to 'immortality'.[18]

Jesus and the kingdom of God

By the turn of the century, however, another fruitful source of controversy was already beginning to emerge. In 1892 Johannes Weiss published *Die Predigt Jesu vom Reiche Gottes* – a book of only sixty-seven pages – which brought Jesus' proclamation of the kingdom of God to the central place in New Testament study which

---

[18] On Conditional Immortality in the nineteenth century see G. Rowell, *Hell and the Victorians*, pp. 180–211. Among the more important studies of judgment and the future life (from various viewpoints) published in English in the next few decades were: S. D. F. Salmond, *The Christian Doctrine of Immortality* (Edinburgh, 1895); F. von Hügel, *Eternal Life* (Edinburgh 1913); H. R. Mackintosh, *Immortality and the Future* (London, 1915); B. H. Streeter *et al.*, *Immortality* (London, 1917); J. H. Leckie, *The World to Come and Final Destiny* (Edinburgh, 1918); J. Baillie, *And the Life Everlasting* (London, 1934).

17

it has held ever since.[19] Nineteenth-century Liberal Protestants such as Adolf von Harnack and Albrecht Ritschl understood the 'kingdom of God' as a religious experience or a moral force in society. Ritschl, for example, wrote: 'The Christian idea of the kingdom of God denotes the association of mankind – an association both extensively and intensively the most comprehensive possible – through the reciprocal moral action of its members.'[20] But Weiss, through comparing the Gospels with Jewish apocalyptic literature, concluded that Jesus' conception of the kingdom was quite different. For Weiss the kingdom was 'always the objective messianic kingdom'.[21] And it was still entirely future. Its shadow had already been cast across the world by the presence of Jesus, but it would come by a future cataclysmic act of God. Gradually Jesus came to realize that it was somehow delayed by the guilt of men. He seized on the audacious and paradoxical idea that his own death at the hands of guilty men would be the means of expiating guilt and causing the kingdom of God to arrive within a generation.[22]

A very similar interpretation was offered a little later by Albert Schweitzer, who apparently reached his conclusions independently of Weiss.[23] According to Schweitzer, Jesus believed himself to be the Messiah-designate. His sending of the twelve on their mission was a last effort to bring about the kingdom (Mt. 10:5ff.). When the kingdom failed to appear he saw that only through his own suffering would the kingdom dawn. Jesus died expecting the immediate dawning of the kingdom and his own coming as Messiah. In this he turned out to be mistaken, and his followers (particularly Paul) transformed his message into a doctrine of two overlapping ages, in which the present age would continue indefinitely until the parousia of Christ.

[19] The English translation by R. H. Hiers and D. L. Holland, *Jesus' Proclamation of the Kingdom of God* (London, 1971) also includes an illuminating discussion by them of the significance and consequences of Weiss's work.

[20] *The Christian Doctrine of Justification and Reconciliation* (ET, Edinburgh, 1908), p. 28.

[21] *Jesus' Proclamation of the Kingdom of God*, p. 133.

[22] See esp. *ibid.*, pp. 81–92.

[23] See *ibid.*, p. 30. There is an interesting discussion of the significance of Schweitzer in D. E. Nineham, 'Schweitzer Revisited', *Explorations in Theology* 1 (London, 1977), pp. 112–133. Handy surveys of eschatological theories from Schweitzer to the present day are G. E. Ladd, *Jesus and the Kingdom* (London, 1966), pp. 3–38 (revised edition entitled *The Presence of the Future* [Grand Rapids, 1974], pp. 3–42); and C. Brown in C. Brown (ed.), *The New International Dictionary of New Testament Theology*, 2 (Exeter, 1976), pp. 901–935. The standard book-length survey is N. Perrin, *The Kingdom of God in the Teaching of Jesus* (London, 1963).

Schweitzer designated his own theory as 'consequente Eschatologie' ('consistent' or 'thorough-going' eschatology), to differentiate it from that of Weiss. He claimed (rather unfairly) that he showed the whole of Jesus' work to be determined by his eschatological beliefs, whereas Weiss concerned himself only with Jesus' preaching.[24]

Despite – or because of – their breakthrough to this eschatological understanding of Jesus, neither Weiss nor Schweitzer felt obliged to insist that Christianity consists in adhering to the teaching of the Christ. They were, as J. W. Bowman puts it, scholars who did not belong to their own school of thought.[25] According to Weiss, 'that which is universally valid in Jesus' preaching, which should form the kernel of our systematic theology is not his idea of the kingdom of God, but that of the religious and ethical fellowship of the children of God.'[26] For Schweitzer, the real subject of Jesus' teaching was love, though it appeared as part of a world-view which expected a speedy end of the world. Schweitzer's own obedience to this conviction led him to depart for West Africa as a medical missionary.[27]

Nevertheless, Weiss and Schweitzer, with their striking interpretation of Jesus' message, set the course for all subsequent study of it.[28] To a great extent, every major twentieth-century interpretation of Jesus' eschatology has been a response to the problem which they identified: the problem of the delay of the parousia. For if they were right in their view that Jesus expected the parousia to follow within a few years (at the most) of his death, then Jesus was mistaken, and the development of thought in the early church has to be understood as a coming to terms with the parousia's non-arrival. Scholars have reacted to the problem in a number of ways.

a. A few scholars have supported Schweitzer's basic approach and

---

[24] See J. Weiss, *Jesus' Proclamation of the Kingdom of God*, pp. 30f. Schweitzer's viewpoint is expounded in the final chapter of his *The Quest of the Historical Jesus* (1906; ET, London, [2]1911); *The Mystery of the Kingdom of God* (ET, London, 1914); *Paul and his Interpreters* (ET, London, 1912); *The Mysticism of Paul the Apostle* (ET, London, 1931); *The Kingdom of God and Primitive Christianity* (ET, London 1968).

[25] 'From Schweitzer to Bultmann', *Theology Today* 11, 1954–5, p. 165.

[26] *Jesus' Proclamation of the Kingdom of God*, p. 135. See also the discussion in *ibid.*, pp. 16–24.

[27] On his view of the relation between Jesus' message and his own theology, see D. E. Nineham, *Explorations in Theology* 1, pp. 129–133.

[28] A valuable critique of Schweitzer's scheme is A. L. Moore, *The Parousia in the New Testament* (Leiden, 1966), pp. 35–48.

have elaborated his thesis that the non-occurrence of the parousia is the key to understanding the development of Christian theology. Martin Werner and Fritz Buri have applied this thesis to the development, respectively, of theology in the first four or five centuries and in more recent theology. Erich Grässer has applied it to the Synoptic Gospels and Acts.[29] But they do not suggest, any more than Weiss and Schweitzer did, that their version of Jesus' message is an appropriate doctrine for Christians to believe today. Buri, for example, opts for 'demythologizing' and for a form of existential interpretation more radical than Bultmann's (on Bultmann, see below, pp. 65ff.).

b. Some other theologians have, despite Weiss and Schweitzer, minimized the importance of eschatology for Jesus' outlook. Adolf von Harnack, the last great Liberal Protestant, maintained in *What is Christianity?* (ET, London, 1901) that although Jesus expected his imminent return, this belief was entirely subservient to his message about the fatherhood of God and the infinite value of the human soul. Similarly E. F. Scott and J. W. Bowman held that apocalyptic eschatology was merely a 'wrapping' or form in which Jesus expressed a message whose content (relationship to God and challenge to repentance) was quite different.[30] A. N. Wilder argued that Jesus' main concern was with a redemption to be worked out in the social-historical future of man. The ethical element is therefore paramount, and Jesus' eschatological teaching is his expression in mythological terms of an ultimate faith in God; cast in this form it adds urgency to his ethical challenge.[31]

c. Another approach is the 'realized eschatology' associated with C. H. Dodd.[32] His view is that Jesus marked a distinctive break with his Jewish apocalyptic background because of his conviction that the kingdom of God was no longer merely an object of expectation, but was actually present in his ministry. In the light of this,

[29] M. Werner, *The Formation of Christian Dogma* (ET, London, 1957 – a shortened version of the 1941 German original); F. Buri, *Die Bedeutung der neutestamentlichen Eschatologie für die neuere protestantische Theologie* (Bern, 1934); E. Grässer, *Das Problem der Parusieverzögerung* (Berlin, 1957).

[30] E. F. Scott, *The Kingdom of God in the New Testament* (London, 1931); J. W. Bowman, *The Religion of Maturity* (Nashville, 1948).

[31] *Eschatology and Ethics in the Teaching of Jesus* (New York, ²1950).

[32] See below, pp. 73ff.

New Testament references to a future coming of Jesus and the consummation of all things must be attributed to the early church's misunderstanding of Jesus and their reversion to apocalyptic. If Jesus did occasionally use the language of apocalyptic mythology, that was merely a picturesque concession to tradition.

A similar emphasis on the present manifestations of the kingdom had been advocated by Rudolf Otto in *The Kingdom of God and the Son of Man* (1934, ET, London, ²1943), though for him eschatology was not so completely 'realized' as for Dodd.

This approach was further developed by T. F. Glasson and J. A. T. Robinson, both of whom attempted to explain how and why the early church's hope of a future coming of Jesus might have arisen.[33]

d. Rudolf Bultmann accepted in principle the view of Weiss and Schweitzer that Jesus proclaimed the imminence of an apocalyptic kingdom. But he interpreted the significance of Jesus' message in a quite different way from them.[34] For him the crucial thing about Jesus' ministry and proclamation of the kingdom was that it created a crisis demanding a decision. 'The future element in the proclamation is not so much temporal as existential; it is future in the sense that it is coming towards men and demanding a decision of them.'[35] Bultmann thus claimed to reach the heart of Jesus' message by demythologizing it in the categories of Heidegger's existentialism. Accordingly, the 'de-eschatologized' message of John and the later epistles of Paul, who abandoned emphasis on a temporally future parousia but retained the existential dimension, was the authentic development from Jesus' message. Bultmann's view, then, involves a kind of 'realized eschatology', just as Dodd's involves an element of 'demythologizing'.

Pupils of Bultmann, such as G. Bornkamm, H. Conzelmann, E. Fuchs, E. Käsemann and the American J. M. Robinson, have been more willing than he was to acknowledge that the kingdom of God was in some sense present in Jesus' ministry. But they have repeated his insistence that the existential reference, rather than the temporal, is what counts.[36]

e. Oscar Cullmann, W. G. Kümmel and Emil Brunner suggest

---

[33] See below, pp. 79ff.   [34] See below, pp. 65ff.
[35] N. Perrin, *The Kingdom of God in the Teaching of Jesus*, p. 115.
[36] *Ibid.*, pp. 119–129.

that the problem of the delay of the parousia is a problem that has been greatly exaggerated.[37] There are in the New Testament few signs, if any, of the disappointment at the parousia's non-occurrence which is supposed by so many scholars to have troubled the early church. Only three texts (Mt. 10:23; Mk. 9:1; 13:30) explicitly delimit the parousia to a specific time scale. Thus even though in these sayings Jesus was mistaken, and even though the early Christians did not expect history to continue for as long as it has done, the delay caused no great problem for faith. The decisive event, the life, death and resurrection of Christ, had already occurred. This – and not the future coming of Christ at an unspecified date – was the mainspring of Christian life and hope. Nevertheless the future coming, whenever it might occur, remained an integral feature of the scheme of salvation history, marking the completion of the saving process and the beginning of the perfected kingdom of God. The tension between 'already fulfilled' and 'not yet fulfilled' is fundamental for Jesus and the whole New Testament.[38]

f. There are still other scholars who argue for the substantial authenticity of Jesus' eschatological sayings in the gospels, for the reality of the parousia as a future event, and for the view that Jesus was not mistaken in those crucial 'imminence' passages (Mt. 10:23; Mk. 9:1; 13:30). Their view is thus close to that of the scholars reviewed in the previous paragraph, with the same stress on the kingdom as both present and future, except with respect to the 'imminence' sayings. These are interpreted by H. N. Ridderbos as stressing the certainty of fulfilment without delimiting the time (Mk. 13:30), and not as referring exclusively to the parousia.[39] C. E. B. Cranfield, S. S. Smalley and G. E. Ladd see them as being fulfilled

---

[37] See below, pp. 83ff. A similar view is presented in G. R. Beasley-Murray, *Jesus and the Future* (London, 1954); *A Commentary on Mark 13* (London, 1957). In an important article, D. E. Aune agrees that the delay of the parousia was not a problem for the early church, and adds some significant sociological and theological insights into the function of the parousia hope: 'The Significance of the Delay of the Parousia for Early Christianity', in G. F. Hawthorne (ed.), *Current Issues in Biblical and Patristic Interpretation: Studies in Honour of M. C. Tenney* (Grand Rapids, 1975), pp. 87–109.

[38] The view that in Jesus' teaching the kingdom was both present and future is held by many other scholars, *e.g.*, V. Taylor, J. Jeremias, R. H. Fuller, N. Perrin. See N. Perrin, *The Kingdom of God in the Teaching of Jesus*, pp. 79–89, 185–201; also G. E. Ladd, *Jesus and the Kingdom*, p. 35, n. 154 (*The Presence of the Future*, p. 38, n. 161).

[39] *The Coming of the Kingdom* (ET, Philadelphia, 1962), pp. 498–510.

in events such as the fall of Jerusalem which are themselves anticipatory of, and theologically related to, the parousia.[40] Ladd insists
that this perspective is entirely in accord with the tension between
history and eschatology which is characteristic of the Old Testament
prophets. A. L. Moore also thinks they may refer to events anticipatory of the parousia, though he believes that for Jesus the parousia
was in some sense near. He finds in Jesus' understanding of the
future the twin themes of 'eschatology and grace': on the one hand
the end must be near because in the Christ-event it has already begun
to happen, but on the other hand it is delayed to allow men time for
repentance.[41]

The scope of this book

These, then, are some of the issues in eschatology on which attention
has been focused during the last hundred years. There is no denying
the complexity of the problems, to which the variety of solutions
proposed bears adequate witness. But nor can we deny the centrality
of these issues for Christian faith. That is the justification for the
discussion in the following chapters.

Admittedly, there are some very important writers on eschatological issues whose names hardly appear. Some (Karl Barth and Paul
Althaus, for example) are omitted because their main work was done
earlier than 1960. Most of the writings considered here have been
produced in the last twenty years, though I have not aimed at rigid
consistency on this point: in the chapter on the parousia it seemed
important to go back to earlier writings. Some theologians are
omitted from consideration because their views on the issues discussed in this book seem so much part of a larger 'system' that
justice could not be done to them in the space available (Barth again,
Teilhard de Chardin, the Process theologians). So, via what may
seem to be a slightly arbitrary selection of significant theologians,
we shall consider the issues of the parousia of Jesus Christ, life after
death, and divine judgment. But the more I have reflected on those

---

[40] C. E. B. Cranfield, *The Gospel according to St. Mark* (Cambridge, 1963), pp. 287f., 407–9;
S. S. Smalley, 'The Delay of the Parousia', *JBL* 83, 1964, pp. 41–54; G. E. Ladd, *Jesus and the
Kingdom*, pp. 316–320 (*The Presence of the Future*, pp. 320–324).
[41] *The Parousia in the New Testament*, pp. 175–206.

themes the less possible it has seemed to avoid coming to terms with Jewish and Christian apocalyptic, since the New Testament presentation of those themes so often seems to presuppose an apocalyptic perspective. The next three chapters will therefore attempt to assess the significance of apocalyptic for Christian theology.

Before we embark on that study, I wish to draw attention to the basic unity of the various themes to be considered. For it is all too easy to get the impression that 'eschatology' is a rag-bag of assorted, disconnected topics. I shall try to point out how, in the perspective of the New Testament writers, the various topics belong together as different aspects of the completion of God's work of salvation. In other words, the different aspects of eschatology are related to each other because they are all related to Christ. Jewish apocalyptic expectations and attitudes are redefined and redirected in the light of Jesus' mission and message (chapters 2–4). The parousia is central to New Testament expectation precisely because it marks the completion of God's work begun in Christ (chapter 5). Resurrection is the destiny of those who are united with Christ and share in his resurrection (chapter 6). Relationship to Christ is the criterion by which human beings are judged (chapter 7). Christ himself is the distinctive and unifying feature of Christian eschatology.

Chapter Two

Apocalyptic – its rise and significance

The term 'apocalyptic' used to be confined to theological circles, and even there it was used only occasionally and apologetically. But now in the days of polluted oceans and neutron bombs it has become the common property of novelists, film critics and political commentators. E. Rovit writes: 'The metaphor of the Apocalypse is our best model for viewing our contemporary human condition. It alone gives us a large and flexible mythic form that is grand enough to allow a full expression of our agonies and aspirations. What other myth do we possess that is as responsive to the major cataclysms of twentieth century life and death?'[1]

The renewal of scholarly interest in Jewish and early Christian apocalyptic literature has been stimulated partly by the sense of 'doom' felt by many in modern society. But there immediately arises the danger that a superficial search for parallels will produce a distorted view of the similarities between ancient and modern apocalyptic, and that modern ideas and concerns will be read back into the ancient literature.[2] For instance, most modern 'apocalyptic' thinking differs fundamentally from ancient apocalyptic in being God-less, and therefore pessimistic about any possibility of 'salvation' or a new beginning.

[1] 'On the Contemporary Apocalyptic Imagination', *The American Scholar* 37, 1968, p. 463. On apocalyptic themes in modern literature see F. Kermode, *The Sense of an Ending* (New York, 1967). I have myself tried to assess the theological significance of Jewish and early Christian apocalyptic in an article which overlaps partly with chapters 2–4 of this book – see 'The Value of Apocalyptic', *TynB* 30, 1979.

[2] Among scholars sensitive to the parallels between the worlds of ancient and modern apocalyptists are the Americans A. N. Wilder, 'The Rhetoric of Ancient and Modern Apocalyptic', *Interpretation* 25, 1971, pp. 436–453; and P. D. Hanson, *The Dawn of Apocalyptic* (Philadelphia, 1975), pp. 1–4; and the British scholar D. S. Russell, *Apocalyptic: Ancient and Modern* (London, 1978).

But why is it that ancient apocalypticism has only recently become significant in theological discussion? It made a brief appearance by courtesy of J. Weiss and A. Schweitzer at the turn of the century. British scholars such as R. H. Charles and F. C. Burkitt did painstaking work on producing editions and interpretations of the apocalyptic texts.[3] Yet for decades after that apocalyptic literature was regularly ignored. Christian scholars drew a direct line from Old Testament prophets to primitive Christianity, whilst Jewish scholars viewed apocalyptic as sectarian and read back post-AD 70 Judaism into the Hellenistic or even the Persian era.[4] In 1962 E. Käsemann commented: 'Primitive Christian apocalyptic is generally regarded by theological scholars as not being a suitable topic for our day'.[5]

It was in fact Käsemann himself who sparked off the modern discussion of apocalyptic among New Testament scholars with his 1960 essay, 'The Beginnings of Christian Theology'.[6] For several reasons such discussion was overdue. The discovery of the Qumran texts (some of which are of apocalyptic character) in addition to apocalyptic texts already available, provoked the *historical* question: what was the place of this literature and its producers in the development of Israel's faith after the Old Testament period? The question bequeathed by Schweitzer, about the relation between apocalyptic and Jesus and the early church, still demanded a more satisfactory answer. And there was the *theological* question: is apocalyptic a proper development of Old Testament religion? Can an inter-testamental development provide legitimate continuity between the Old and New Testaments? Some systematic theologians have sought to use the apocalyptists' 'philosophy of history' as a basis for their own theology – for example, W. Pannenberg for his concept of 'revelation as history', and J. Moltmann for his 'theology of hope'.[7] It has then fallen to the biblical scholars to debate whether such theologians are

---

[3] On Weiss and Schweitzer and their successors, see above, pp. 17ff. R. H. Charles, *The Apocrypha and Pseudepigrapha of the Old Testament* (2 volumes, Oxford, 1913) is still a standard work. F. C. Burkitt, *Jewish and Christian Apocalypses* appeared in 1914 (London).

[4] F. M. Cross, 'New Directions in the Study of Apocalyptic', in *Apocalypticism*, vol. 6 of *Journal for Theology and the Church*, ed. R. W. Funk (New York, 1969), pp. 159f. (this volume, henceforth referred to as *JTC* 6, contains several important essays). K. Koch, *The Rediscovery of Apocalyptic* (ET, London, 1972), pp. 37, 47, 93, complains that Continental Old and New Testament scholars before the 1970s refused to take Jewish apocalyptic seriously.

[5] 'On the Topic of Primitive Christian Apocalyptic', *JTC* 6, p. 100.

[6] See below, pp. 41ff.   [7] See below, pp. 50ff., 56ff.

using the apocalyptic texts in a legitimate manner, or are imposing their own theological system on alien material. It is clearly time we considered the nature of the material with which the debate is concerned.

The problem of defining 'apocalyptic'

Defining 'apocalyptic' is comparable to defining 'socialism'. If I am aiming at a definition of 'socialism', should I define it by reference to socialist literature or party manifestos? Or should I describe it in terms of the attitudes of those who still remember vividly and bitterly the unemployment during the Depression? Should I assume that western democratic socialism is basically the same thing as the socialism of a Marxist state? Or should I treat their use of the same word, 'socialism', as little more than coincidence? Does it make any difference whether I spell the word with a capital or small 's'?

Similarly, there is no simple way of defining 'apocalyptic'. It has to be approached on several levels.

a. Literary genre. The term 'apocalyptic' derives from Revelation 1:1, where the Greek word *apokalypsis* is used to describe the literary genre of John's book. It is an 'unveiling' of 'what must soon take place', given by God through his angel to John. The term 'apocalypse' has thus come to be used to describe other books – Jewish and Christian – which purport, by revelations through visions, dreams or angels, to describe the heavenly world and God's plan for the future. But 'apocalypse' was not used as a title for any Jewish book of this type (it appears in the titles of 2 and 3 Baruch, but is a later addition). 'Apocalyptic' cannot be defined solely in terms of literary genre because there are many books, such as the Testaments of the Twelve Patriarchs, which have some 'apocalyptic' ideas, but are in a quite different literary form. And other literary features often regarded as characteristic of apocalyptic, such as pseudonymity, are not peculiar to this body of literature.

b. Doctrinal features. Books are commonly designated as apocalyptic if they bear features such as the following: pessimism about the course of history; dualism between God and Satan, between the earthly world and the heavenly world, between the present age and the age to come; prediction of future events leading to an imminent end of history; faith in the triumph of God; belief in resurrection and final judgment.[8] A definition in terms of such themes brings us closer to the 'heart' of apocalyptic. But it is still imprecise, since no one Jewish or early Christian book contains all these features. How many does a book have to have in order to be classified as 'apocalyptic'? Are some features more fundamental than others?

c. *Sociological milieu*. An increasing number of scholars are saying that what gives unity to such a diverse body of literature is the social and historical situation in which it was produced.[9] The 'ethos' reflected in the literature may be a more important indication of its being 'apocalyptic' than its precise form or list of contents.

Recent study has made the problem of definition more complex. Although it has not made any easier the task of deciding whether, say, the Book of Jubilees should be labelled 'apocalyptic', it has at least reduced the danger of superficial and wrong judgments based on one-sided evidence. We should not, in any case, expect to find a foolproof way of determining what literature is apocalyptic and what is not: who would claim to know *precisely* when a 'gospel' is not a gospel, or when 'science fiction' is not science fiction? Any system of classification in the world of thought or literature involves some blurring at the edges. With caution, then, we may accept D. S. Russell's list of Jewish books 'generally accepted as apocalyptic or having apocalyptic elements'.[10] His list includes the biblical book of Daniel, the apocryphal 2 Esdras (= 4 Ezra), fifteen non-canonical works and several of the Qumran Scrolls. In addition we could mention certain passages in the Old Testament prophets which lean towards an apocalyptic eschatology (to be considered in a moment), and in the New Testament the Revelation to John and certain other passages such as Mark 13 and 2 Thessalonians 2.

[8] For fuller lists of literary and doctrinal features, and discussion of their significance, see K. Koch, *The Rediscovery of Apocalyptic*, pp. 24ff.; D. S. Russell, *The Method and Message of Jewish Apocalyptic* (London, 1964), pp. 104ff.; P. Vielhauer in E. Hennecke and W. Schneemelcher, *New Testament Apocrypha* 2 (ET, London, 1965), pp. 582ff.; L. Morris, *Apocalyptic* (London, 1973), pp. 34ff.

[9] On the milieu of apocalyptic, see further, below, pp. 29ff.

[10] *The Method and Message of Jewish Apocalyptic*, pp. 37ff. The task of defining apocalyptic more precisely is advanced by various attempts to identify different *types* of apocalyptic. *E.g.*, Hengel distinguishes between early (Hasidic) apocalyptic and its later elaborations (*Judaism and Hellenism* [ET, London, 1974], 1, pp. 189f.); R. W. Bauckham distinguishes 'eschatological' from 'cosmological' apocalypses ('The rise of Apocalyptic', *Themelios* 3.2, January 1978, p. 17).

28

The origin and milieu of apocalyptic

An earlier generation of scholars confidently asserted that apocalyptic developed out of the prophetic movement. Thus H. H. Rowley claimed: 'That apocalyptic is the child of prophecy, yet diverse from prophecy, can hardly be disputed'.[11] And S. B. Frost concluded: 'In general, prophecy shifted its eschatological interest from the outworking of history to the end of time itself, and re-emerged as apocalyptic.'[12] We shall return to this, but must first note some counter-proposals.

a. Ever since the rise of the 'History of Religions' school at the beginning of this century, it has been noted that there are parallels in *Parseeism* to several doctrines of Jewish apocalyptic – dualism, universalism and individualism, resurrection of the dead, predetermined periodically-structured course of history, influence of evil in this good world and eschatological victory of the good.[13] Such ideas could have filtered through into Jewish thought during the two centuries after 539 BC when Persian influence in Palestine was strong. It would be idle to deny that Parseeism had some influence on the rise of apocalyptic. But it cannot be the dominant factor, since what appear to be some of the most crucial elements of Jewish apocalyptic – its pessimism about the present age, its expectation of an imminent end, its stern denial that all men will be saved – are not found in Parseeism.

b. G. von Rad has argued that apocalyptic is a development from the *Wisdom literature*. He notes, for instance, that both wisdom and apocalyptic literature are concerned not so much with Israel as a nation but with the individual and his place among all men; that wisdom's 'encyclopaedic interest' in such things as cosmology, astrology, biology, angelology reappears, for example, in 1 Enoch; that apocalyptic's deterministic view of history corresponds to Eastern wisdom-thought, which ascribes a fixed time to every event; and that both apocalyptic and wisdom are concerned with theodicy, *i.e.*,

[11] *The Relevance of Apocalyptic* (London, ³1963), p. 15.
[12] *Old Testament Apocalyptic* (London, 1952), p. 83.
[13] See W. Schmithals *The Apocalyptic Movement* (ET, Nashville, 1975), pp. 113–118. H. Conzelmann thinks 'Persian influence is determinative' for apocalyptic: *An Outline of the Theology of the New Testament* (ET, London, 1969), p. 23.

vindicating the righteousness of God in the face of evil and suffering.[14]

Again, there is something in this view. But its treatment of the persistent eschatological interest of apocalyptic is woefully inadequate. And von Rad overlooks the fact that, apart from 1 Enoch, there is rather little of the 'encyclopaedic wisdom' on which his thesis leans.[15]

c. H. D. Betz sees Jewish apocalyptic as one strand of a much wider movement in the *Hellenistic world.* From a survey of parallel ideas in Hellenistic and oriental literature he concludes that 'Jewish and, subsequently, Christian apocalypticism as well cannot be understood from themselves or from the Old Testament alone, but must be seen and presented as peculiar expressions within the entire development of Hellenistic syncretism'.[16] M. Hengel also presents numerous Hellenistic parallels to apocalyptic themes, but believes that Hellenism influenced the apocalyptists only in matters of detail, not in their basic faith.[17] Betz's suggestion of 'syncretism' is therefore misleading; his chosen method of study does demonstrate similarities on a rather limited front, but minimizes the differences which derive from the apocalyptists' historical experiences and from the nature of their God.

It seems clear, therefore, that any one-sided view of the derivation of apocalyptic is wrong. But there are strong reasons for reaffirming the view that apocalyptic developed from Old Testament prophecy, particularly in its understanding of history and eschatology. P. D. Hanson suggests that the development took place in the following way.[18]

---

[14] *Old Testament Theology,* 2 (ET, Edinburgh, 1965), pp. 306–308. The discussion is expanded in the fourth German edition (Munich, 1965, not in ET). See the discussion in W. Schmithals, *The Apocalyptic Movement,* pp. 128–131.

[15] In an incisive survey, Bauckham describes and assesses a refined version of the wisdom hypothesis, whereby a distinction is made between 'mantic wisdom' (reflected in Daniel's interpretation of dreams) and 'cosmological wisdom' (*cf.* 1 Enoch's 'encyclopaedic interests') (*Themelios* 3.2, pp. 10–23).

[16] 'On the Problem of the Religio-Historical Understanding of Apocalypticism', *JTC* 6, p. 155.

[17] *Judaism and Hellenism,* 1, pp. 181–194.

[18] This summary is derived mainly from Hanson's article 'Apocalypticism', *Interpreter's Dictionary of the Bible: Supplementary Volume* (Nashville, 1976), pp. 28–34, especially pp. 32f. But see also P. D. Hanson, *The Dawn of Apocalyptic,* and *idem,* 'Old Testament Apocalyptic Reexamined', *Interpretation* 25, 1971, pp. 454–479; and R. J. Bauckham's discussion of P. D. Hanson, *Themelios* 3.2, pp. 10–12.

The pre-exilic prophets took history seriously as the realm of God's activity, and declared that he would fulfil his covenant promises of salvation and judgment on the plane of history. But the community crisis and national disintegration caused by the exile led Jeremiah (4:23–28), Ezekiel (ch. 47), and then especially Second Isaiah to portray redemption increasingly on a cosmic level. Through re-application of ancient myths (*e.g.* Is. 51:9–11) Second Isaiah described the cosmic drama of salvation and introduced the dichotomies between heaven and earth, and between the past age and the future age (43:18f), which become central in later apocalyptic. But Second Isaiah's optimistic sense of nationhood enabled him to integrate this cosmic vision with historical realities (45:1–8).

The followers of the tradition of Second Isaiah found themselves increasingly oppressed by the holders of political power, and their hopes shifted irrevocably from the historical, political sphere to the supra-historical realm. 'Thus the apocalypticism of their symbolic universe was predicated upon the disintegration of the present order and the creation of a new cosmic order of blessedness for the elect. Responsibility to the political order which was a central characteristic of prophetic eschatology was abandoned in favour of a new supermundane universe of meaning.'[19] Hanson believes that Old Testament passages originating from this movement between the exile and 400 BC are Isaiah 34–35; 24–27; 56–66; Malachi; Zechariah 9–14; and perhaps Joel.

In these passages we already find ideas typical of later apocalyptic eschatology: judgment and salvation are not for the nation as a whole but respectively for the faithless and the faithful within Israel.[20] There is a doctrine of *universal* judgment.[21] Eschatology takes on *cosmic* dimensions: a new act of creation will introduce a radically different age beyond the judgment.[22] This development involved the revivification of ancient mythical material, especially the Divine Warrior myth, to portray the coming eschatological triumph of Yahweh.[23]

Ezra then introduced a period of greater stability and harmony within the nation, which caused the apocalyptic spirit to lie dormant.

---

[19] P. D. Hanson, *Interpreter's Dictionary of the Bible: Supplementary Volume*, pp. 32f.
[20] *The Dawn of Apocalyptic*, pp. 143f., 150f.   [21] *Ibid.*, pp. 185, 207.
[22] *Ibid.*, pp. 155–161, 376–379, 397.   [23] *Ibid.*, pp. 300–323, 328–333.

But when the violent oppression of Antiochus IV Epiphanes in the second century created an overwhelming sense of alienation, circles like the early *hasidim* ('pious ones') responded to this situation in the manner of the earlier apocalyptic movements. 'The struggles of this earth were only shadows of battles occurring between the princes of heaven, and the outcome was certain to favor the elect (Dn. 10:10–21).'[24] Whilst the successes of the Maccabees led some groups to channel their energies into political reconstruction, other groups such as the monks of Qumran 'withdrew further into the symbolic universe of apocalypticism'. From such groups the bulk of extant apocalyptic books emerged.[25]

With this historical reconstruction Hanson supports his claim that the transcendent eschatology which characterizes apocalyptic arose among the post-exilic prophets in response to the historical situation of the post-exilic community. It was an internal development within the prophetic tradition, not fundamentally affected by influences from outside Israel or from outside prophecy. His reconstruction is speculative since we have very little solid evidence about the nature of the Israelite community after the exile. And it assumes a post-exilic dating for parts of Isaiah and a second-century dating for Daniel. If one assigns Daniel to the sixth century, one could still agree with Hanson that the main pressure leading to apocalyptic thought was the sense of oppression and alienation provoked by great historical crises; and that the two 'high points' of apocalyptic literary activity were the century from about 550 to about 450 BC and the period of upheaval provoked by Antiochus IV Epiphanes in the second century. But Daniel would belong to the earlier of these two periods, whilst the non-canonical apocalypses such as 1 Enoch are products of the latter period.[26] Hanson, and other recent writers

[24] *Interpreter's Dictionary of the Bible: Supplementary Volume*, p. 33.

[25] *Ibid.* For brevity's sake I have had to simplify his historical reconstruction. It has some affinities with the widely acclaimed thesis of O. Plöger that from the fifth century to the second the successors of the prophetic movement were overshadowed by the 'theocratic' strand in Israel's life which believed that God's promises were already fulfilled in a community founded on cult and law; but, Plöger argues, in the crisis provoked by Antiochus Epiphanes, this 'minority movement' sprang to life again as the 'hasidic' movement and produced the book of Daniel (*Theocracy and Eschatology* [ET, Oxford, 1968]).

[26] See J. G. Baldwin, *Daniel: an Introduction and Commentary* (Leicester, 1978), pp. 35–46, for arguments in favour of the view that Daniel was written around 500 BC; and pp. 46–59 for a valuable discussion of the origins of apocalyptic and Daniel's relation to the apocalyptic tradition. See *NBD*, pp. 572–574 for arguments for and against a sixth century dating for Is. 40–66.

such as J. G. Baldwin, have convincingly reasserted the old view that the roots of apocalyptic are in Israelite prophecy. There are already signs of an apocalyptic transcendent eschatology in the early post-exilic prophets, but this transcendent eschatology did not reach its fully developed form until the period when most of the apocalypses were produced – 200 BC to AD 100.

Against the background of this reconstruction, the following 'theses' about the rise of apocalyptic may be suggested.

a. The post-exilic community witnessed a *decline* in prophetic activity. Although there were a few prophets in the early post-exilic period, whose books appear in the Old Testament, Zechariah 1:4 suggests that the prophets themselves sensed that prophecy was not what it used to be.[27] Psalm 74:9 – 'There is no more any prophet' – is also often quoted in this connection.

b. But the process of *interpretation* of older prophecies went on within the prophetic-apocalyptic movement.[28] So, for example, Daniel 9:2 interprets the 'seventy years' of Jeremiah. The apocalyptists were especially concerned with the continued non-fulfilment of earlier prophetic predictions – predictions of a golden age ushered in by 'the day of Yahweh', promises that evil and oppression would end, that the nations would flock to Jerusalem, that a God-sent deliverer would reign for ever, that in a new heaven and new earth righteousness and peace would rule.

c. The problem of unfulfilled prophecy was not academic for the apocalyptists, since they were a minority element in Jewish society. They were 'the disenfranchised' 'men without power'.[29] Several writers echo Hengel's description of the 'conventicle-like segregation of the "pious" from the official cult community'.[30] Their sense of

[27] See D. S. Russell, *The Method and Message of Jewish Apocalyptic*, p. 74. On pp. 73–82 he discusses further evidence for this decline in prophecy and suggests reasons for it. P. Vielhauer, however, produces evidence to show that during the period 200 BC – AD 200 there were, contrary to common opinion, numerous Jewish prophets – of a kind (*New Testament Apocrypha*, 2, pp. 601–605).

[28] M. Hengel, *Judaism and Hellenism*, 1, p. 206; D. S. Russell, *The Method and Message of Jewish Apocalyptic*, pp. 178–202. NB also that the author of the Johannine Apocalypse regarded himself as a prophet (Rev. 1:3, 22:10, *etc.*).

[29] P. D. Hanson, *Interpretation* 25, p. 474; L. Morris, *Apocalyptic*, p. 73.

[30] *Judaism and Hellenism*, 1, p. 180. Citing 1 Enoch 93:9, Hengel notes that its author regarded the whole of 'official Israel' since the exile as thoroughly apostate. On the 'conventicle' nature of apocalyptic religion *cf.* W. Schmithals, *The Apocalyptic Movement*, pp. 45f.; O. Plöger, *Theocracy and Eschatology*, pp. 26–52.

alienation reached a crisis-point at the time of Antiochus IV's oppression. But it would be wrong to suppose that, once the Antiochan crisis was over, times became easy for them so that their continued 'conventicle mentality' was a pure anachronism. It does not require even their rigorist attitude to sense that the whole period from the Maccabean revolt to Bar Kochba's revolt of AD 132–5 was one of blood and tears.[31]

d. In this situation, and confronted by unfulfilled prophecies, the apocalyptists were preoccupied with *theodicy:*[32] how could God be said to be working out his saving purpose when the subjection of his faithful people went on unabated? Was not the exile sufficient punishment for Israel's sins? How is faith to react when the imperfections of the present time become intolerable?

e. This combination of prophetic tradition and historical circumstances provoked the break-up of the old prophetic hope of God's activity on the historical plane, and led to apocalyptic's distinctive *transcendent eschatology.* If salvation was to come, it could not be on the historical level, but must arise from the intervention of God to bring a new, transcendent reality. Thus the old prophetic tension between divine activity and historical reality 'snapped'. From one angle, the door was opened to let in a mixed bag of fantastic and unhelpful cosmological speculations. But from another angle, apocalyptic was responding in a legitimate way to the limitations of prophecy, rather as Job and Ecclesiastes responded to the limitations of Proverbs. Apocalyptic eschatology was after all an affirmation of faith – faith in the covenant God who would come soon to vindicate his people.

However, it must be stressed that this distinction between prophetic eschatology as 'historical' and apocalyptic eschatology as 'transcendent' is a generalization – a useful one, but one which has been overworked especially by those eager to disparage apocalyptic as compared with prophecy. The true situation is more complex, as

---

[31] M. Hengel, *Judaism and Hellenism*, 1, p. 194, *pace* W. Schmithals, *The Apocalyptic Movement*, pp. 148f. *Cf.* M. Knibb's demonstration that numerous Jewish apocalyptists took the view that Israel's exile continued long after the sixth century, and would be ended only by God's intervention in this world order to establish his rule ('The Exile in the Literature of the Inter-Testamental Period', *Heythrop Journal* 17, 1976, pp. 253–272).

[32] This is one of apocalyptic's links with wisdom literature – though they tackled the problem in different ways.

we shall see in the next section.

Apocalyptic history and eschatology

Most modern assessments of apocalyptic take its attitude to history as the crucial test of acceptability. The claim is frequently made that whereas the prophets affirmed God's saving activity in history, the apocalyptists could envisage the possibility of salvation only by abandoning history and pinning their hopes on a totally new era brought about through God's intervention. And if the claim is true, it is implied, so much the worse for apocalyptic. This negative conclusion is based mainly on four prominent aspects of apocalyptic thought.

a. Pessimism about the course of history. This is evident in the apocalyptists' theory that in this age the world is not ruled by God but is given over into the control of demonic forces (*e.g.*, the 'princes' of Dn. 10–12; 1 Enoch 89:61 and *passim*); and in the fact that they have no political programme and very little ethical exhortation. They thus assume no responsibility for history.[33] The glorious age to come will not arise out of history but will break into it from beyond.

b. The course of history is *predetermined* (*e.g.*, Dn. 11:36; 2 Esdras 4:36f.; 6:1–6). 'The dynamic of a history which is the living out of a genuine covenant relationship yields to the inflexibility of a history which becomes a timetable of cosmic events'.[34] Many apocalypses express this conviction by their systematic arrangement of history into fixed periods. By the pseudonymous device of presenting their historical surveys as predictions of an ancient sage, they are able to give the impression that all history conforms to God's predetermined plan, and that the imminent climax of history has been revealed to them. History from creation to end is surveyed in 1 Enoch 85–90, in the 'Ten Weeks' Apocalypse' (1 Enoch 93:1–10; 91:12–17) and 2 Baruch 53–74. Other passages present surveys of shorter periods, *e.g.*, from the exile to the end (Dn. 2, 7, 8–12; 2 Baruch 36–40; Testament of Levi 16–18).[35] Thus the apocalyptists

---

[33] *Cf.* W. Schmithals, *The Apocalyptic Movement*, pp. 45f., 80f.

[34] P. D. Hanson, *Interpretation* 25, pp. 478f. *Cf.* D. S. Russell, *The Method and Message of Jewish Apocalyptic*, pp. 230–234; M. Hengel, *Judaism and Hellenism*, 1, pp. 181–189.

[35] For more examples see P. Vielhauer, *New Testament Apocrypha*, 2, pp. 585f.

have systematized what the prophets glimpsed: the whole of history, of which Israel is only a part, is the sphere of a coherent divine plan.

This might be thought to indicate that the apocalyptists have a very positive view of history. But many scholars argue quite the opposite. W. R. Murdock, in an important critique of the Pannenberg circle's interpretation of apocalyptic, argues that, since many of the surveys only cover recent history and the time of the readers is always located just before the eschaton, the purpose of the surveys is not to present a theology of history but to promote imminent expectation of the end of history. The historical surveys are subservient to the dualistic distinction between the present age – when evil forces rule – and the age to come.[36] Therefore God does not reveal himself in history, according to the apocalyptists, but in their apocalyptic literature.[37]

c. There is a sharp *dualism* between the present evil age and the age to come (*e.g.*, 2 Esdras 7:50).[38] Since there is no continuity between the two ages (2 Baruch 31:5), history is meaningless: it is not going anywhere.

d. The belief in an *imminent* end of this age – a belief which persisted from Daniel (*e.g.*, Dn. 12:11) right through to 2 Baruch in the late first century AD (*e.g.*, 2 Baruch 85:10), despite its non-fulfilment – also betrays an abandoning of responsibility and hope for the present historical age. All hope is focused on the coming glory of God, which will wipe away history.[39]

All of this seems to leave room for only one answer to von Rad's question 'whether apocalyptic literature had any existential relationship with history at all, since it had abandoned the approach by way of saving history. This question', he writes, 'must be directed to the very conception from which apocalyptic literature gains its splendour; that of the unity of world history.' Again he asks 'whether history has not been excluded from the philosophy which lies behind this gnostic idea of epochs that can be known and calculated, a philosophy which has dispensed with the phenomenon of the con-

---

[36] 'History and Revelation in Jewish Apocalypticism', *Interpretation* 21, 1967, pp. 170f. *Cf.* P. D. Hanson, *Interpretation* 25, pp. 477f.
[37] *Interpretation* 21, pp. 180–6.
[38] See, *e.g.*, P. Vielhauer, *New Testament Apocrypha*, 2, pp. 588f., and pp. 590f., where he suggests that dualism and determinism are the two outstanding characteristics of the apocalyptic thought-world.   [39] *Cf.* P. Vielhauer, *ibid.*, pp. 590–593.

tingent'. Such features 'mark the great gulf which separates apocalyptic literature from prophecy'.[40]

However, a convincing case for assessing more positively the
apocalyptic understanding of history and eschatology has been presented by Bauckham, whose argument I now summarize.[41]

The negative view described above derives from hasty generalization, and a selection of proof-texts from later rather than earlier
apocalypses and of texts closer to Persian dualism rather than those
most influenced by Old Testament prophecy. Moreover, it betrays
a lack of sympathy for the desperate circumstances of the apocalyptists and their problem of theodicy. They did not begin with a dogma
about the nature of history (that God cannot act in the history of
this world), but with 'an empirical observation of God's relative
absence from history *since the fall of Jerusalem*'. It was of this period
of history that they took a negative view; this is the period (not the
whole of history) embraced by Daniel's four world empires. The
idea in 1 Enoch 89:59 – 90:17 that the seventy 'shepherds' commis-
sioned to rule Israel during this period exceed their brief and allow
the righteous to suffer oppression, is a crude way of coping with the
same problem.

This view of post-exilic history came to a head under Antiochus
Epiphanes. The apocalyptic movement's longing for God's intervention on behalf of the faithful was 'not a retreat from history but
precisely an expectation that God would vindicate his people and his
justice on the stage of history, though in such a way as to transcend
ordinary historical possibility'. In the absence of prophets, and in
the face of fear that God had abandoned his people, the apocalyptists
reasserted the prophetic faith – even if some of them indulged in
rather too much speculation.

Because of post-exilic Israel's historical involvement with world
empires, and because of their vision of God's triumph over every
form of evil – including death – it is understandable that the apocalyptists should resort to the language of 'new creation' to describe
the expected act of God which would greatly transcend his acts in
the past. Thus arose their temporal dualism though the terminology
of two ages does not appear until the first century AD. 'This is

[40] *Old Testament Theology*, 2, pp. 304–306.   [41] *Themelios* 3.2, pp. 19–23.

significant because it shows that apocalyptic did not begin from a dualistic dogma, but from an experience of history.' Hence the contrast between two ages is never absolute: God's action in Israel's past is stressed, for example, in 1 Enoch 85–90.[42] Because they believed he had acted in the past they hoped for his action in the future, though their present experience made the hope of total transformation the only appropriate expression of faith in a God who rules history. Prophetic faith could only survive the post-exilic experience by giving birth to eschatological faith. We may be grateful for that despite the danger that it might lead to despair about God's activity in all history.

The hasidic apocalyptists do not seem to have been so 'quietist' as is normally supposed. Since 1 Enoch 90:8–18 regards the Maccabean victories as the beginning of God's eschatological victory, and since the book of Daniel was preserved and canonized even though the 'age to come' did not arrive, it seems likely that apocalyptic hope mobilized support for the Maccabees, and their victories were viewed as provisional realizations of God's promises. Transcendent eschatology, far from emptying history of divine action, can help interpretation of God's action in history. This is not to claim that the apocalyptists always maintained this tension between history and eschatology. In the end they did not: as a result of the traumas of AD 70 we find 2 Esdras taking a very negative view of all history from Adam to the end of this age, and presenting a stark dualism between the two ages.

Bauckham agrees that the apocalyptists speak of history as predetermined, in a manner quite different from the prophetic conception in which Yahweh makes continually fresh decisions (*cf.* Je. 18:7–10). But he asserts that their viewpoint remained quite distinct

---

[42] K. Koch also stresses that apocalyptic dualism is not an absolute dualism, observing that sometimes the rule of God is thought of as already present, though concealed (Dn. 4:3; 2 Esdras 7:26ff.) (*The Rediscovery of Apocalyptic*, p. 31). NB also that the common generalization – that apocalyptists envisaged the age to come or the messianic kingdom in a transcendent world discontinuous with this world – is quite misleading. There was a variety of expectations, and a number of apocalypses from Daniel onwards seem to expect an earthly-historical kingdom, though in conditions of blessedness which make it radically different from the present age. As late as 2 Esdras and 2 Baruch (both after AD 70) the tension between an earthly and a totally transcendent kingdom remained unresolved, as can be seen from the 'compromise' solution in which they envisage a temporary earthly kingdom followed by an eternal transcendent one. On this issue see D. S. Russell, *The Method and Message of Jewish Apocalyptic*, pp. 266–271, 285–297.

from their pagan neighbours' resignation to fate, since, alongside a passage like Daniel 11, with its determinism, they were able to place a passage like Daniel 9, with its conviction that God judges his people for their rebellion and responds in mercy to their repentance and to the prayers of intercessors like Daniel.[43] Positively, apocalyptic determinism served to support eschatological faith in the face of the negative experience of history. The emphasis on God's sovereignty relativizes the power of pagan empires (note the thoroughly prophetic idea in Daniel 2:21 that it is God 'who removes kings and sets up kings'), and stresses that in the last resort the promise of eschatological salvation is *un*conditional (as it was indeed for the prophets, such as Second Isaiah). Apocalyptic determinism actually counters fatalistic despair, lays open to men the eschatological future, and calls them to appropriate action.[44]

Thus the apocalyptists' 'transcendent eschatology was both a solution, in that the problem of history demands a solution which transcends history, and an aggravation of the problem, as apocalyptic hopes remained unfulfilled'. This apocalyptic framework of belief formed an essential bridge to the New Testament, which also rests on the conviction that the meaning of human life and history is ultimately to be found beyond the history of this world.[45] The New Testament writers avoided the apocalyptists' tendency to a negative evaluation of history not because they reverted to a prophetic, pre-apocalyptic understanding of salvation history,[46] but because in Jesus 'the apocalyptic expectation had entered a phase of decisive fulfilment': God had already acted in an eschatological way.

Thus far Bauckham. But his last-mentioned remarks already anticipate our next section. Before moving on, however, we must note

---

[43] M. Hengel also insists on the difference between apocalyptic determinism and Hellenistic resignation to fate (*Judaism and Hellenism*, 1, pp. 195, 209).

[44] That ethical concern is present in the apocalypses is argued by D. S. Russell, *The Method and Message of Jewish Apocalyptic*, pp. 100–103; and P. Vielhauer, *New Testament Apocrypha*, 2, p. 587. It is hardly surprising that we do not find the same measure of ethical preaching as in the pre-exilic prophets: which of us, if writing to friends suffering persecution, would spend most of our time on moral exhortation? But we might encourage them to faithfulness and endurance, as the stories in Dn. 1, 3, 6 do.

[45] The basic truth of this insight of apocalyptic is emphasized also by H. H. Rowley, *The Relevance of Apocalyptic*, p. 171; D. S. Russell, *The Method and Message of Jewish Apocalyptic*, pp. 223f.

[46] *Contra* W. G. Rollins, 'The New Testament and Apocalyptic', *NTS* 17, 1970–71, pp. 454–476.

that it was the apocalyptists who introduced to Israel the belief in resurrection and judgment after death.[47] It is curious how some scholars who regret the apocalyptists' abandonment of history in favour of transcendent eschatology should apparently not even give them credit for bringing into prominence these beliefs which have been so central in the Judeo-Christian tradition. They are scarcely mentioned in von Rad or Hanson. The beliefs about resurrection and judgment took many forms – clearly there was no 'orthodoxy' on these matters in pre-Christian Judaism.[48] But these convictions – thrust upon the apocalyptists as they looked for the justice of God in the face of extreme sufferings – were a very significant affirmation that the meaning of human existence cannot be discovered entirely within life and history.

In this chapter we have seen that there are good reasons for believing that, even though Jewish apocalyptic literature has some affinities with wisdom literature and with certain strands of non-Jewish thought, the apocalyptic movement had its main roots in the prophetic tradition. The transcendent eschatology characteristic of apocalyptic began to appear in the prophets of the exile; the ensuing century (about 550–450 BC) witnessed further developments; and – after a period when the apocalyptic spirit was mostly dormant – apocalyptic writers were again active between 200 BC and AD 100. Attention has been drawn to the importance, for the apocalyptists, of belief in resurrection and final judgment, topics which will concern us again in chapters 6 and 7. And it has been argued that the apocalyptists were not so negative in their attitude to the present course of history as some scholars claim. In the next chapter we shall see how the early Christians' conviction that apocalyptic expectations were coming to decisive fulfilment in Jesus Christ affected their use of apocalyptic language. In particular, we study how Jesus' own attitude to apocalyptic has given to apocalyptic ideas a permanent and significant place in Christian theology.

---

[47] See D. S. Russell, *The Method and Message of Jewish Apocalyptic*, pp. 353–390.
[48] See M. Hengel, *Judaism and Hellenism*, 1, pp. 196–202; and the full studies of G. W. E. Nickelsburg, Jr, *Resurrection, Immortality, and Eternal Life in Inter-Testamental Judaism* (Cambridge, Mass., 1972); H. C. C. Cavallin, *Life After Death: Paul's Argument for the Resurrection of the Dead in 1 Cor. 15. Part I: an Enquiry into the Jewish Background* (Lund, 1974). R. J. Bauckham has an important note arguing that a doctrine of general rewards and punishments after death already appears in 1 Enoch 22, a pre-Maccabean passage (*Themelios* 3.2, p. 17, n. 45).

Chapter Three

Apocalyptic, Jesus and early Christianity

Ernst Käsemann and his critics

How significant was apocalyptic eschatology for Jesus and the first Christians? Ever since A. Schweitzer produced his picture of a thoroughly apocalyptic Jesus, it has been common for scholars to react by arguing that Jesus himself did not think in apocalyptic terms, but that the earliest Christian church did. This view was taken by W. Bousset.[1] It recurs in E. Käsemann's 1960 essay, 'The Beginnings of Christian Theology', which has given rise to a spate of articles, mostly critical, by Continental, British and American authors.[2]

Käsemann's thesis is that 'post-Easter apocalyptic is the oldest variation and interpretation of the kerygma';[3] and that 'apocalyptic . . . was the mother of all Christian theology'.[4] Jesus preached 'the nearness of God' in a *non-apocalyptic* way, and was opposed to apocalyptic teaching on ethics and the law, the nature of God and calculations about the time of the end.[5] But the Easter event and the

---

[1] *Die jüdische Apokalyptik, ihre religionsgeschichtliche Herkunft und ihre Bedeutung für das neue Testament* (Berlin, 1903). Important passages from the book appear in English in W. Kümmel, *The New Testament: the History of the Investigation of its Problems* (ET, London, 1973), pp. 260–262. On this whole aspect of interpretation see chapter 6 of K. Koch's *The Rediscovery of Apocalyptic* (ET, London, 1972), provocatively entitled 'The Agonised Attempts to Save Jesus from Apocalyptic: Continental New Testament Scholarship'.

[2] E. Käsemann's original essay, with contributions by other scholars and a further essay by Käsemann, appears in English in *JTC* 6, ed. R. W. Funk (New York, 1969). Käsemann's two essays are also translated in his *New Testament Questions of Today* (London, 1969), pp. 82–107, 108–137.

[3] 'On the Topic of Primitive Christian Apocalyptic', *JTC* 6, p. 107, n. 5.

[4] 'The Beginnings of Christian Theology', *JTC* 6, p. 40.

[5] *JTC* 6, pp. 40, 115f.

coming of the Spirit provoked the first Christians to formulate their theology in apocalyptic terms. Käsemann's arguments for this viewpoint include the following.[6]

a. From certain texts in Matthew's Gospel which, he believes, derive not from Jesus but from the post-Easter church, he postulates the existence within the early church of a vigorous Jewish-Christian group, led by prophets and marked by typically apocalyptic traits. These include (1) a theology of history which sees the history of salvation and the history of damnation running parallel to each other, which divides history into 'clearly distinguishable epochs', and which asserts that the epoch of the end and the epoch of the beginning of time correspond to each other (Mt. 24:37);[7] (2) ethical exhortations which appeal to an eschatological *ius talionis* (*i.e.* the principle of 'an eye for an eye' or 'tit for tat', *e.g.*, Mt. 7:2; 13:12; 23:12; 25:29);[8] (3) expectation of a transformation of values (*e.g.*, Mt. 10:26, 39) in the last days;[9] (4) re-establishment of the twelve tribes at the parousia;[10] (5) confirmation of the Mosaic law and opposition to the gentile mission;[11] (6) 'hope of the epiphany of the Son of Man coming to his enthronement' and 'near expectation of the parousia'.[12]

b. This apocalyptic theology collapsed, according to Käsemann, when the imminently expected parousia failed to materialize.[13] But it left Christian theology in its debt in that it (1) made historical thinking possible within Christianity; and (2) thus gave rise to the formation of a gospel history and the narration (rather than mere announcement) of the kerygma of Jesus; (3) most importantly, its central hope of 'the epiphany of the Son of Man' provoked the question 'whether Christian theology can ever make do, or be legitimate, without this motif which arose from the experience of Easter and determined the Easter faith.'[14]

c. As Christianity spread beyond Palestine, Hellenistic enthusiasm, such as Paul encountered at Corinth, transformed apocalyptic to such an extent that it abandoned 'any kind of theologically relevant

---

[6] A fuller summary can be found in W. G. Rollins, 'The New Testament and Apocalyptic', *NTS* 17, 1970–71, pp. 455–458.
[7] *JTC* 6, pp. 33f.   [8] *JTC* 6, pp. 29f., 32, 36, 45.   [9] *JTC* 6, p. 37.
[10] *JTC* 6, p. 45. Käsemann never actually explains on what evidence in the text he bases this assertion.
[11] *Ibid.*   [12] *JTC* 6, p. 46, and p. 100, n. 1.   [13] *JTC* 6, p. 45.   [14] *JTC* 6, pp. 34f., 46.

future hope at all'.[15]

d. Paul represents a mid-point between 'post-Easter apocalyptic' and 'Hellenistic enthusiasm'.[16] He continued the apocalyptic strand of thought, for example, in his insistence against Corinthian 'enthusiasts' that God's plan of salvation still awaits future realisation; in his doctrine of 'God's righteousness' and 'our justification'; and in his description of the future eschatological realm as *basileia Christi* ('kingdom of Christ').[17]

But in opposition to post-Easter apocalyptic Paul distinguishes 'between the church as the redeemed creation and the world as the unredeemed creation' (a modification of the apocalyptic 'two ages' doctrine); and stresses that the Christian life cannot be 'restricted to inwardness and cultic celebrations'.[18]

Reaction against Käsemann has been surprisingly vigorous. Several scholars have questioned his view that apocalyptic thought dominated the earliest post-Easter church. In a critique published in 1961, G. Ebeling takes Käsemann to task for failing to define what he means by 'apocalyptic', and he expresses his own suspicions about apocalyptic when he points out, firstly, that in the theological tradition of the Reformation apocalyptic is regarded as the first step to heresy.[19] Käsemann's reply to the request for a definition is in terms of 'near expectation of the parousia' and 'the special kind of eschatology that would seek to speak of the end of history'.[20] But it can hardly be denied that his use of the term remains fuzzy.

Secondly, Ebeling observes that if primitive Christianity were as indebted to Jewish apocalyptic as Käsemann claims, it is surprising that the Christian production of apocalypses was a *late* development. 'It is no accident that the characteristic literary form of Christianity was the gospel and not the apocalypse.'[21]

Thirdly, Ebeling criticizes Käsemann for not taking enough

---

[15] *JTC* 6, p. 119.　　[16] For this paragraph see *JTC* 6, pp. 126–130.

[17] *Cf. JTC* 6, p. 44. Käsemann is concerned to stress, against Bultmann, that 'God's righteousness' in Paul refers to God's triumph in the world rather than to merely individual salvation. *Cf.* ' "The Righteousness of God" in Paul', *New Testament Questions of Today*, pp. 168–182, esp. pp. 180–182. *Cf.* K. Koch, *The Rediscovery of Apocalyptic*, p. 77.

[18] *JTC* 6, p. 130.

[19] 'The Ground of Christian Theology', *JTC* 6, pp. 50f.

[20] *JTC* 6, p. 100, n. 1. See further W. G. Rollins, *NTS* 17, pp. 458f.

[21] *JTC* 6, p. 53.

account of the way apocalyptic ideas have themselves been changed through their association with Jesus. We should not 'merely interpret Jesus in the light of apocalyptic, but also and above all interpret apocalyptic in the light of Jesus' – just as we do not simply understand Jesus in the light of Jewish concepts of 'Messiah', but rather we understand the meaning of 'Messiah' (Christ) in the light of Jesus.[22] In reply, Käsemann agrees that when speaking of apocalyptic he means 'apocalyptic modified by faith in Jesus'.[23] But perhaps even this concedes too much to Ebeling. For no Jew of Jesus' time could have recognized Jesus as Messiah without *some* prior understanding of what 'Messiah' means, however much that understanding might be modified by actual encounter with Jesus. And the same goes for apocalyptic.

Fourthly, Ebeling points to the inherent difficulty in explaining how the supposedly non-apocalyptic preaching of Jesus could be countered, or supplanted, by apocalyptic preaching. Käsemann's suggestion that the Easter event and the coming of the Spirit provoked the early church's apocalyptic proclamation is inadequate because it fails to explain why an apocalyptic response to those events should be regarded as a response to the life and message of *Jesus*.[24]

Finally, Ebeling's own lack of sympathy for apocalyptic is revealed in his long quotation from Kierkegaard, which compares the true believer to an oarsman. Just as the oarsman rows with his back to the goal, so the believer turns his back on his eternal goal and lives out his faith today. And 'it is the believer who is nearest the eternal, while the apocalyptic visionary is farthest from the eternal.'[25] Käsemann accepts the importance of present tasks, but drily remarks that oarsmen find coxes – who *have* got their eye on the goal – useful to prevent them from following a false or zig-zag course.[26]

E. Fuchs accuses Käsemann of minimizing the element of 'realized' eschatology in primitive Christianity (*e.g.*, Acts 2:36). And he argues that even if apocalyptic was the initial form of Christian response, that does not prove it to be a permanently valid response. [27]

But the main difference between Fuchs and Käsemann arises from

[22] *JTC* 6, p. 58.   [23] *JTC* 6, p. 107, n. 6.   [24] *JTC* 6, pp. 58f.
[25] *JTC* 6, pp. 65f.   [26] *JTC* 6, p. 101.
[27] 'On the Task of a Christian Theology', *JTC* 6, pp. 70–72.

their different dogmatic premises. Fuchs criticizes apocalyptic for expressing itself in terms of propositional truths, since he believes that revelation cannot be identified with propositional truths.[28] Käsemann, on the other hand, asks: 'But preaching, confession, and even hermeneutics without stated truths, and even without "conceptions" – what is that supposed to mean?'[29] Propositions, in some form, are essential if revelation is to occur. Among other critics of Käsemann, R. Bultmann has suggested that 'not apocalyptic, but eschatology is the mother of primitive Christian theology.' By that he means, of course, the eschatology of the present (rather than futurist eschatology), interpreted in an existentialist framework.[30]

W. G. Rollins repeats some of the criticisms of Käsemann which we have already noted, and adds others.

a. Käsemann's use of texts from Matthew is arbitrary: nowhere does he present arguments to justify his claim that these texts reflect the theological tensions of the earliest church. What evidence we have (e.g., from 1 Cor. 15) suggests that earliest forms of the kerygma did not use apocalyptic concepts such as Son of man and parousia.[31] Even if the texts cited by Käsemann indicate the existence of an apocalyptic 'strand' or apocalyptic groups in the primitive church, they hardly demonstrate that apocalyptic was the controlling theological attitude of the earliest church. It was 'not the mother of all Christian theology, but at best one of many brothers, whose particular brand of theology would have stood in obvious tension with the teaching of Jesus and the theology of the earliest church.'[32]

b. Changing the metaphor yet again, Rollins says that the role of apocalyptic was not that of mother but that of midwife. The Christ-event itself was what produced the theologies of the first Christians;

[28] JTC 6, pp. 81f.

[29] JTC 6, p. 113, n. 12. A further discussion of the arguments of Ebeling and Fuchs is in K. Koch, The Rediscovery of Apocalyptic, pp. 78–82.

[30] 'Ist die Apokalyptik die Mutter der christlichen Theologie?', in Apophoreta. Festschrift für E. Haenchen, ed. W. Eltester (Berlin, 1964), pp. 64–69; reprinted in Bultmann's Exegetica (Tübingen, 1967), pp. 476–482. On Bultmann's interpretation of eschatological language, see below, pp. 65ff.

[31] NTS 17, p. 465, citing R. W. Funk, 'Apocalyptic as an Historical and Theological Problem in Current New Testament Scholarship', JTC 6, pp. 185 f. Cf. H. Conzelmann, 'On the Analysis of the Confessional Formula in 1 Cor. 15:3–5', Interpretation 20, 1966, pp. 15–25.

[32] NTS 17, pp. 468, 470f.

45

Jewish apocalyptic supplied only a mode of conceptualizing the Christ-event.[33]

c. In proclaiming Jesus as Messiah, the early church reclaimed history and the world as the locus of God's self-disclosure, thus displacing the pessimism of Jewish apocalypticism. Rollins interprets this as 'a tacit rejection of Jewish apocalyptic eschatology and a return to prophetic Heilsgeschichte'.[34]

d. From the earliest beginnings of the church there was opposition to apocalyptic. What should surprise us is not that we find apocalyptic material in the New Testament, but that we find so little of it. Rollins lists the book of Revelation, Mark 13 and parallels, Luke 17:20–37, and 'scattered fragments of "apocalyptic-looking" material': 1 Corinthians 15:20–28; 2 Corinthians 12:4; Ephesians 3:3f.; 1 Thessalonians 4:13 – 5:6; 2 Thessalonians 1:4–10; 2:1–12; Hebrews 12:22–29; James 5:7–11, 1 Peter 1:13ff.; 2 Peter 3; 1 John 2:18–28; 4:1–6; 2 John 7. In any case, none of these passages can be traced to the earliest church, and even within these sections there are some 'anti-apocalyptic elements', such as the rejection of calculation of the end by means of signs in Mark 13:32; Luke 17:20f. Therefore 'one can speak of the "apocalypticism" of the New Testament only with extreme caution'.[35]

All these criticisms raise important issues, and help to correct a certain vagueness and arbitrariness which seems to characterize Käsemann's presentation. Yet there are two fundamental weaknesses – one in Käsemann's own argument and one in the viewpoint of most of his critics – which must now be pinpointed.

Jesus and apocalyptic

Käsemann postulates a double discontinuity in his argument that though John the Baptist and the earliest church were apocalyptists, Jesus himself was not. Admittedly, Käsemann shares this position

[33] NTS 17, p. 472.
[34] NTS 17, p. 473.
[35] NTS 17, pp. 475f. Rollins' list of texts of course minimises the influence of apocalyptic concepts on the New Testament. For instance, it ignores the apocalyptic background of terms such as 'resurrection', 'Son of man' and 'kingdom of God'; and Paul speaks of the parousia in several texts besides the ones cited. For a slightly fuller survey of apocalyptic texts in the New Testament, see P. Vielhauer, New Testament Apocrypha, 2, pp. 608–626.

with other scholars associated with the 'New Quest of the Historical Jesus'. All the same, it is hard to imagine anything more improbable. Not surprisingly, Koch suspects that this concern to preserve Jesus from apocalyptic has more to do with modern antipathy towards futurist eschatology or salvation-history than with 'objective' historical research.[36]

J. D. G. Dunn observes especially the following apocalyptic features in Jesus' teaching.[37]

a. Jesus probably used the language of the two ages (*e.g.*, Mk. 3:29; 10:30). His more characteristic phrase 'the kingdom of God' is not a regular apocalyptic phrase,[38] but is in fact a variation on the two-ages motif – his way of speaking about the age to come (*e.g.*, Mt. 6:10; 8:11). The discontinuity between the two ages is marked in various ways, particularly by the fact that the final judgment will mark the beginning of the age of the kingdom (Mt. 19:28).

b. He anticipated the time of eschatological trial prior to the end (*e.g.*, Mt. 5:11f.; 6:13).

c. He seems to have thought of the end as imminent (*e.g.*, Mk. 1:15; 9:1; 13:30).

d. He probably saw the climax of the end events as the coming from heaven of (himself as) the Son of man, deliberately echoing the apocalyptic language of Daniel 7 (*e.g.*, Mk. 8:38).[39]

e. Jesus' technical term 'the kingdom *of* God' underlines his belief

---

[36] *The Rediscovery of Apocalyptic*, pp. 83f., 127; *cf.* pp. 68f. on the 'New Quest' theologians.

[37] *Unity and Diversity in the New Testament* (London, 1977), pp. 318–322. The authenticity of some texts cited as evidence by J. D. G. Dunn, and the apocalyptic nature of some of the concepts described, have been disputed from time to time. To debate such details, important though they are, is beyond the scope of this study. Let it merely be said here that Dunn's conclusions derive from widely accepted criteria for establishing the probable authenticity of words of Jesus; and that a survey of the views of scholars on both sides of this debate about Jesus and apocalyptic may be found in K. Koch, *The Rediscovery of Apocalyptic*, esp. pp. 57–97.

[38] But the notion of a kingdom given to God's people is important in Dn. 7, as in the teaching of Jesus.

[39] The apocalyptic background to the term 'Son of man' in the Gospels has been disputed by R. Leivestad, 'Exit the Apocalyptic Son of Man', *NTS* 18, 1971–72, pp. 243–267; G. Vermes, *Jesus the Jew: a Historian's Reading of the Gospels* (London, 1973), pp. 160–191. But against them see B. Lindars, 'Re-enter the Apocalyptic Son of Man', *NTS* 22, 1975–76, pp. 52–72; M. D. Hooker, 'Is the Son of Man Problem Really Insoluble?', in E. Best and R. McL. Wilson (eds.), *Text and Interpretation: Studies in the New Testament Presented to Matthew Black* (Cambridge, 1979), pp. 155–168. And on the Background and authenticity of the Son of man sayings see I. H. Marshall, *The Origins of New Testament Christology* (Leicester, 1976), pp. 63–82.

both in its transcendent character, and in God's sovereign control of events leading to its full establishment.

This evidence justifies Dunn's conclusion that 'Jesus' expectation of the future kingdom was apocalyptic in character', and that Käsemann's hypothesis of 'such a complete discontinuity between an *apocalyptic* John the Baptist, a *non*-apocalyptic Jesus, and an *apocalyptic* primitive community is scarcely credible'.[40]

Apocalyptic transformed

As Dunn is eager to point out, however, Jesus did not simply take over Jewish apocalyptic unchanged. He modified it, by rejecting the practice of drawing up a calendar of the end-time, and particularly by claiming that the eschatological kingdom was *already* present through his ministry.[41] This brings us to the second weakness, the weakness in Käsemann's critics.

Several of them stress how the early Christians modified apocalyptic motifs in the light of Jesus' impact upon them, just as Dunn observes Jesus' own modifications of apocalypticism. Rollins, for example, refers to Jewish apocalyptic's sense of the meaninglessness of history, and then contrasts it with the positive evaluation of history and of the world which arises from the early church's realized eschatology. He views the New Testament as 'the product of a post-apocalypticism, rooted in the experience of Easter and Pentecost, which from the beginning represented a theological orientation in fundamental conflict with Jewish apocalypticism'. So the church was delivered from the follies of apocalyptic, and returned to the wiser ways of the prophets, with their affirmation that God discloses himself in present history.[42]

[40] *Unity and Diversity in the New Testament*, pp. 321, 322.
[41] *Ibid.*, p. 321. I do not myself think that the drawing up of calendars was ever a very prominent exercise among apocalyptists. See L. Hartman, 'The Functions of Some So-called Apocalyptic Timetables', *NTS* 22, 1975–76, pp. 1–14; and my comments in 'The Value of Apocalyptic', *TynB* 30, 1979.
[42] *NTS* 17, pp. 454, 473. *Cf.* S. Laws, 'Can Apocalyptic be Relevant?' in M. D. Hooker and C. Hickling (eds.), *What about the New Testament?: Essays in Honour of Christopher Evans* (London, 1975), pp. 96–101. More plausible is the thesis of G. E. Ladd, that the prophetic and apocalyptic perspectives are not as different as is sometimes supposed, that Jesus' eschatology was basically apocalyptic but that he recovered the prophetic positive view of the present age, which the apocalyptists had lost ('Why Not Prophetic-Apocalyptic?', *JBL* 76, 1957, pp. 192–200).

But this method of unfavourably comparing apocalyptic on the one hand with Old Testament prophecy and New Testament realized eschatology on the other misconstrues the relationship between them. What Rollins calls the 'post-apocalypticism' of the New Testament does not arise from a rejection of apocalyptic and a reversion to a prophetic attitude, but rather from a recognition that the expectations of the apocalyptists have begun to find their fulfilment in Jesus.[43] Of course the atmosphere of the New Testament is very different from that of the Jewish apocalyptic writings. But it is different not because Jesus and his first followers rejected apocalyptic but because they took it for granted. Unless there had first developed an apocalyptic eschatology, with its hope of a radically different new age and resurrection from the dead, there would not have been the message of Jesus and the apostles that we find in the New Testament. Our conclusion, then, is that the apocalyptic eschatology has a more positive place in the New Testament than either Käsemann or many of his critics allow. Käsemann is wrong to postulate a non-apocalyptic Jesus and an apocalyptic early church. His critics are wrong when they deny the importance of apocalyptic for Jesus' first followers as well as for Jesus himself. Dunn seems to be much nearer the truth in his claim that Jesus *accepted* apocalyptic expectations and *transformed* them because in him they had become expectations-in-process-of-fulfilment. This perspective of expectation-coming-to-fulfilment was followed by the writers of the New Testament.[44] Chapter 5 will discuss more fully the nature of that fulfilment.

---

[43] This perspective is hinted at, but not made explicit, in W. G. Rollins, *NTS* 17, p. 466; S. Laws, *What About the New Testament?*, pp. 97–100. It is more explicit in W. Schmithals, *The Apocalyptic Movement*, pp. 158f., and in R. J. Bauckham, *Themelios* 3.2, p. 22.

[44] On the grounds that the Johannine Apocalypse maintains this perspective, G. R. Beasley-Murray is able to defend its character as a Christian book, in 'How Christian is the Book of Revelation?', in R. J. Banks (ed.), *Reconciliation and Hope, Essays Presented to L. Morris* (Exeter, 1974), pp. 275–284.

Chapter Four

Apocalyptic and systematic theology

Wolfhart Pannenberg

Ever since Schweitzer the debate about apocalyptic has reflected a widespread reluctance to allow that apocalyptic thought may have any contribution to make to dogmatic or systematic theology. But in 1959 a young German systematic theologian (then unknown to the world) announced a theological programme for which apocalyptic concepts were central. Pannenberg's essay 'Redemptive Event and History' began with the statement: 'History is the most comprehensive horizon of Christian theology'.[1] In opposition both to the existential theology of Bultmann, which dissolves history into an individual, subjective affair, and to the traditional theology of 'salvation history', which places 'saving history' on a different level of reality from ordinary, 'external' history, he proposed a bold new 'eschatological theology of history'.[2] Surprising though it may seem to anyone unfamiliar with or unsympathetic towards Pannenberg's approach, this 'eschatological theology of history' goes hand in hand with his emphasis on rationality. His complaint against the 'theology of the Word' advocated by Barth and Bultmann is that it is based not on rational argument but on an authoritarian appeal to revelation. This stress on the need for faith to be built on reasoned argument rather than authoritarian proclamation also commits him to rigorous

---

[1] Translated in *Basic Questions in Theology*, 1 (London, 1970), p. 15.

[2] Some of Pannenberg's major writings are referred to in the following footnotes. Useful general surveys of his thought are A. D. Galloway, *Wolfhart Pannenberg* (London, 1973); E. F. Tupper's more detailed *The Theology of Wolfhart Pannenberg* (London, 1974); and the collection of essays in *New Frontiers in Theology*, 3, *Theology as History*, ed. J. M. Robinson and J. B. Cobb, Jr (New York, 1967). The present chapter is concerned only with Pannenberg's use of apocalyptic.

historical-critical research and to its results.

Pannenberg affirms that history is the sphere of God's self-revelation.[3] But (he says) real, complete revelation cannot be given by any particular 'bit' of history, and must therefore be placed at the end of history, when history can be viewed as a whole. How then can we, who still live in the stream of history, have access to the end of history? Pannenberg's answer is that in Jesus Christ the character of the end of history has been made known: 'In the fate of Jesus of Nazareth, God has been revealed to all men.'[4] 'The witness of the New Testament is that in the fate of Jesus Christ the end is not only seen ahead of time, but is experienced by means of foretaste. For, in him, the resurrection of the dead has already taken place, though to all other men this is still something yet to be experienced.'[5] Pannenberg speaks of Jesus' resurrection as *prolepsis* ('foretaste', 'anticipation') of the end of history.

Pannenberg found support for these conclusions in Jewish apocalyptic and its use by the early church. Leaning on D. Rössler's controversial book, *Gesetz und Geschichte*, he stressed that the apocalyptists were the first to give systematic expression to the idea of universal history. In particular, their surveys of history from creation to the end indicate their view of history 'as a whole', in which God reveals himself partially and indirectly in his historical acts, but only at the end will he be finally and fully revealed as the one and only God.[6]

Moreover, the apocalyptists' view of history included not only the whole of time but also the whole world. 'Salvation history' is broadened to become 'universal history'. 'This corresponds completely to the universality of Israel's God, who is not only the God of Israel,

---

[3] See, *e.g.*, 'Dogmatic Theses on the Concept of Revelation', in *Revelation as History* (ET, London, 1969), pp. 123–158. This volume of essays by Pannenberg, with R. Rendtorff, T. Rendtorff and U. Wilckens, appeared in 1961. They, along with other scholars such as K. Koch and D. Rössler, formed what became known as the 'Pannenberg circle'. But Pannenberg has denied being the leader of the group or the originator of all its main ideas. See *Revelation as History*, p. 200, n. 1.

[4] *Revelation as History*, p. 138.

[5] *Ibid.*, p. 141. *Cf.* E. F. Tupper's discussion of this concept in *The Theology of Wolfhart Pannenberg*, pp. 92–94.

[6] *Ibid.*, pp. 132f. On D. Rössler's work, *Gesetz und Geschichte: Untersuchungen zur Theologie der jüdischen Apokalyptik und der pharisäischen Orthodoxie* (Neukirchen, 1960), see K. Koch, *The Rediscovery of Apocalyptic*, (ET, London, 1972), pp. 40–42, 85–90.

but will be the God of all men.'[7]

As for his thesis that Jesus is the anticipatory revelation of God, Pannenberg justifies it on the ground that apocalypticism linked the revelation of God's glory at the end with the general resurrection of the dead; therefore the resurrection of Jesus, understood in an apocalyptic context, anticipates the final resurrection and revelation. Indeed, Jesus' resurrection is inconceivable apart from its apocalyptic context: 'It is only within this tradition of prophetic and apocalyptic expectation that it is possible to understand the resurrection of Jesus and his pre-Easter life as a reflection of the eschatological self-vindication of Jahweh.'[8] Admittedly, Jesus' resurrection breaks apocalyptic expectation (because it is the resurrection of one man, *before* the general resurrection at the end of history), but it can be understood only within the apocalyptic tradition.[9] Pannenberg's well-known claim that the resurrection of Jesus can be historically verified is not our concern here.[10] But we can see how important it is for him once we have grasped how central the resurrection is for his understanding of revelation, and how concerned he is to resist the 'flight from history' which he detects in some twentieth-century existential theologies and 'theologies of the Word'.

Pannenberg does not subscribe to the common view that apocalyptic thought is hopelessly foreign and irrelevant to modern man. 'Although the apocalyptic concept of the end of the world may be untenable in many details, its fundamental elements, the expectation of a resurrection of the dead in connection with the end of the world and the Final Judgment, can still remain true even for us.' Indeed, 'if the apocalyptic expectation [of the end of history] should be totally excluded from the realm of possibility for us, then the early Christian faith in Christ is also excluded'. Christology would become mythology – something quite different from the message of Jesus and the apostles.[11]

[7] *Revelation as History*, p. 133.
[8] *Ibid.*, p. 127; cf. p. 193. On the significance of Jesus' resurrection see further the six points made by Pannenberg in *Jesus – God and Man* (ET, London, 1968), pp. 66–73.
[9] See E. F. Tupper, *The Theology of Wolfhart Pannenberg*, p. 104.
[10] See W. Pannenberg, 'Did Jesus Really Rise from the Dead?', in R. Batey (ed.), *New Testament Issues* (London, 1970), pp. 102–117; *Jesus – God and Man*, pp. 88–106; and the discussion in E. F. Tupper, *The Theology of Wolfhart Pannenberg*, pp. 151–160, 274–285.
[11] *Jesus – God and Man*, pp. 82f.

This allusion to 'mythology' draws attention once again to a major reason for the prominence of apocalyptic in Pannenberg's scheme: its concern for history, he believes, stands in opposition to the 'demythologizing' kind of theology which refuses to take history seriously. He goes on to stress that the apocalyptic expectation of the resurrection of the dead is crucial, because 'the question is inescapable whether the individual may expect a fulfilment of his destiny as man beyond death, or whether the question about man's humanity must simply be regarded as meaningless'.[12] The dimension of future fulfilment beyond this world and its history, as expressed in apocalyptic thought, is indispensable if meaning is to be discovered for history and for the life of the individual.

Before drawing attention to some criticisms of Pannenberg we must note – what his critics sometimes fail to observe – that he claims to use apocalyptic categories as they were *modified by Jesus*. Although he sometimes makes risky generalizations about apocalyptic, he aims to focus his thought on Christ, the anticipatory fulfilment of apocalyptic expectations, rather than make indiscriminate use of pre-Christian apocalypses.[13]

Pannenberg's interpretation of apocalyptic has been criticized particularly in three ways.

a. Questions have been raised about the notion of 'universal history' in apocalyptic. W. R. Murdock argues that Pannenberg has been misled by Rössler in his view that universal history was a central concern of the apocalyptists.[14] Very few apocalypses in fact include surveys of history from creation to the end: most of them begin with more recent history (*e.g.*, Dn. 2; 2 Baruch 36–40). Nor is it at all obvious that the purpose of these surveys is to present a theology of history or to speak of revelation in history. Their purpose seems rather to be to promote imminent expectation of the end. The determinism in these historical surveys does not express God's control and self-revelation in events, but rather the fact that for a fixed period the world, including Israel, has been delivered into the control of the demonic powers.[15] The radical break between this

---

[12] *Ibid.*, p. 84.
[13] See E. F. Tupper, *The Theology of Wolfhart Pannenberg*, pp. 134–137; A. D. Galloway, *Wolfhart Pannenberg*, pp. 62–69.
[14] 'History and Revelation in Jewish Apocalypticism', *Interpretation* 21, 1967, pp. 167–187.
[15] *Ibid.*, pp. 168–171.

age and the age to come means that the age to come cannot be the 'goal' of history in a positive sense, but only its 'end' in a merely negative way.[16] Finally, Murdock argues that the apocalyptists' concept of revelation is not one of revelation in history (since their view of history is pessimistic), but of revelation in their apocalyptic literature. And that is a very different conclusion from Pannenberg's.[17]

I have already argued, however, that the view of history in apocalyptic is rather more positive than Murdock thinks.[18] And yet it is hard to believe that the apocalyptists would have shared Pannenberg's view that the whole of history reveals God, and that therefore the end of history will be the complete revelation of God *because* all history will then have happened. They surely thought of the end more as a great new act of God, like (but transcending) his earlier acts of salvation and judgment, but also pronouncing God's 'no' over the evil in history. Pannenberg's scheme of revelation through the whole of history has difficulty in allowing for this element of contradiction and condemnation of evil in history. On the other hand, it is hard to be sure how far Pannenberg needs to find *precisely* his view of revelation as history in the apocalyptists. It may be sufficient that they, like him, had some sense of the significance of universal history and looked to the end of history for its meaning. Murdock, then, by raising questions demanding further clarification, may have dented Pannenberg's armour, but has not knocked him down.

b. S. Laws has questioned whether apocalyptic had any genuine universal hopes. Is it not more likely, she suggests, that the history of other nations is told simply to provide the context of Israel's redemption, or even to represent that from which she is redeemed?[19] To this it may be replied, firstly, that some Jewish apocalyptists certainly entertained hopes of salvation for Gentiles;[20] and secondly,

---

[16] *Ibid.*, pp. 175–179.

[17] *Ibid.*, pp. 179–187. With Murdock's criticisms, *cf.* those of H.-D. Betz, 'The Concept of Apocalyptic in the Theology of the Pannenberg Group', *JTC* 6, pp. 192–207.

[18] Above, pp. 37–39. See further K. Koch, *The Rediscovery of Apocalyptic*, pp. 90f.; E. F. Tupper, *The Theology of Wolfhart Pannenberg*, pp. 270f. G. I. Davies has recently warned that, in the present state of knowledge, it is unwise for anyone to be dogmatic about *why* the apocalyptists wrote about history ('Apocalyptic and Historiography', *Journal for the Study of the Old Testament*, 5, January 1978, pp. 15–28).

[19] 'Can Apocalyptic be Relevant?', in M. D. Hooker and C. Hickling (eds.), *What about the New Testament?* (London, 1975), p. 92.

that early Christian apocalyptic surely transcends Jewish nationalism and attains universal scope.

c. On the issue of the resurrection, it is difficult to separate criticisms of Pannenberg's argument about the apocalyptic context of Jesus' resurrection from other criticisms about its place in Pannenberg's theological scheme.[21] But two comments are appropriate. First, whilst it is true that New Testament statements about the resurrection do not make sense apart from their apocalyptic background, Pannenberg pays inadequate attention to the great variety of hopes about life after death in Jewish inter-testamental literature.[22] Secondly, in making the Jewish apocalyptic expectation of a resurrection from the dead a *presupposition* for the recognition of Jesus' resurrection and for an understanding of its meaning, Pannenberg 'does not take adequate account of the fact that Judaism did not anticipate resurrection as a *decisive event* in history, nor of the fact that in its happening the resurrection of Jesus radically transformed the whole concept of resurrection.'[23]

The validity of Pannenberg's 'system' must of course be judged on much wider considerations than are possible here. Admittedly, the apocalyptic basis of his scheme may not be entirely secure. But we have seen enough to justify Koch's claim that 'Pannenberg's scheme is without question the only one at the moment which makes it possible to assimilate theologically the apocalyptic trends of the period between the Testaments, with their view of history and their expectation of the end.'[24] Pannenberg has argued more comprehensively than any other twentieth-century theologian that a genuinely futurist eschatology is essential for Christianity. 'The decisive reason why Christianity cannot do without an eschatology is that the reconciliation of the world, the presence of God, and his kingdom through Christ, have taken place only in the form of an anticipation of a future which in its fullness has not yet materialized.'[25]

---

[20] See D. S. Russell, *The Method and Message of Jewish Apocalyptic*, pp. 297–303.

[21] See, *e.g.*, K. Koch, *The Rediscovery of Apocalyptic*, pp. 105f.; E. F. Tupper, *The Theology of Wolfhart Pannenberg*, pp. 274–276, 280–285.

[22] Even in *Jesus – God and Man*, pp. 74–81, where he does discuss several apocalyptic texts.

[23] T. F. Torrance, *Space, Time and Resurrection* (Edinburgh, 1976), p. 34, n. 10.

[24] *The Rediscovery of Apocalyptic*, p. 106.

[25] 'Can Christianity do without an Eschatology?', in *The Christian Hope*, by G. B. Caird *et al.* (London, 1970), p. 30.

Jürgen Moltmann

Whilst Pannenberg's work is more comprehensive in scope, Moltmann's is even more insistently future-oriented than Pannenberg's. In the introduction to his *Theology of Hope* he announces his programme: 'There is . . . only one real problem in Christian theology . . .: the problem of the future.'[26] What matters is the future of Jesus Christ himself, whose resurrection has set in motion a developing process extending to the parousia. Hence 'the eschatological is not one element *of* Christianity, but it is the medium of Christian faith as such'.[27] Christianity as 'the religion of expectation' concerns the future not merely of individuals but of the whole cosmos.

A prominent theme in Moltmann's writing is expressed thus: 'The theologian is not concerned merely to supply a different interpretation of the world, of history and of human nature, but to transform them in expectation of a divine transformation.'[28] Hence his emphasis on mission, finely expounded in the final section of *Theology of Hope*, entitled 'Exodus Church'. Christians' hope for the future is not for themselves only, but is to be shared with the whole of society. The church is 'like an arrow sent out into the world to point to the future.'[29] Its mission involves both the proclamation of the gospel and the socio-political struggle for justice and liberation.

The significance of apocalyptic for Moltmann is rather different from its significance for Pannenberg – an indication that the study of ancient apocalyptic has not yet produced clear-cut results on which systematic theologians may confidently draw. Three points in Moltmann's scheme may be noted.

a. Whereas Pannenberg stresses the concept of universal history leading towards its goal in the age to come, Moltmann makes use of apocalyptic's radical discontinuity between the present and future

[26] *Theology of Hope: On the Ground and the Implications of a Christian Eschatology* (ET, London, 1967), p. 16. Admittedly, this enormous stress on the future is balanced by other emphases in his more recent books, *e.g.*, on the cross of Jesus in *The Crucified God* (ET, London, 1974).

[27] *Theology of Hope*, p. 16.

[28] *Ibid.*, p. 84. Presumably Moltmann is deliberately echoing Karl Marx's words at the end of his *Theses on Feuerbach*: 'The philosophers have only interpreted the world differently; the point is to change it.'

[29] *Ibid.*, p. 328.

ages. Christian hope is indeed born of this contradiction between present and future, between historical reality and the promise expressed in Jesus' resurrection.[30] Apocalyptic thus becomes the symbol of revolutionary change. As Koch says in his comparison of Moltmann with Pannenberg: 'Where the one scents revolution – which is to say rupture and discontinuity – for the other evolution, that is, progress and continuity, seems to be the guiding aim.'[31]

b. Apocalyptic is not concerned only with individuals, but with the cosmos. '. . . The now universal hope for history would here be setting the cosmos in motion. . . . The "universe" is no longer, as in pagan cosmology, a thing to be interpreted in astro-mythical or pantheistic or mechanistic terms as the sum total of the world and of our satisfaction with it. Instead, it splits into aeons in the apocalyptic process – into a world that is coming and one that is passing away. . . . The whole world is now involved in God's eschatological process of history, not only the world of men and nations. . . . Without apocalyptic a theological eschatology remains bogged down in the ethnic history of men or the existential history of the individual.'[32] This view of apocalyptic is obviously related to Moltmann's insistence that the church's mission has to do not merely with individuals but with the non-human – or supra-human – structures of society, with matters of politics and economics.

c. Contrary to the usual stress on the determinism of apocalyptic, Moltmann works with the concept of an 'open future'. In apocalyptic, he suggests, 'it might well be that the existing cosmic bounds of reality, which the moving historic horizon of the promise reaches in eschatology, are not regarded as fixed and predetermined things, but are themselves found to be in motion. . . . The *eschaton* would not be a repetition of the beginning, . . . but is ultimately wider than the beginning ever was.'[33] The biblical word of promise 'already creates something new. . . . The expectation of fulfilment remains

[30] *Ibid.*, pp. 18f. On Moltmann's understanding of apocalyptic, see esp. *ibid.*, pp. 133–138.
[31] *The Rediscovery of Apocalyptic*, p. 108. For a list of other differences between Moltmann and Pannenberg, see E. F. Tupper, *The Theology of Wolfhart Pannenberg*, pp. 257–261. Paradoxical though it may seem, throughout history apocalyptic thought has frequently been a stimulus to revolutionary activity and political change: see the survey in W. Schmithals, *The Apocalyptic Movement*, pp. 213–248.
[32] *Theology of Hope*, pp. 137f.
[33] *Ibid.*, p. 136.

open for moments of *surprise*.[34] God as 'the power of the future' sets men free 'creatively to seize the new possibilities of the future'.[35] There is something dynamic, even exciting, about Moltmann's way of approaching the future. But – whilst there is not yet a book-length appraisal in English of his thought – he has not escaped criticism for his handling of apocalyptic.[36]

a. Koch welcomes the all-embracing scope of Moltmann's eschatology, but complains that his vision of the radical discontinuity between present and future is unsatisfactory because it is asserted rather than developed and explained. 'In the interests of his inclination towards a revolutionary ideology, Moltmann in the end tears salvation and creation apart, which is neither apocalyptic nor reasonable.'[37] I have shown above that the discontinuity is not so great in most Jewish apocalypses as his scheme would suggest.[38] Also, his tendency to use biblical imagery of the *eschatological* future with reference to the future *within history* obscures the biblical and apocalyptic distinction between the two. 'Hope' for Moltmann is a historical hope, not a transcendent one – we shall note in chapter 6 that he seems not to accept belief in life after death.[39] In this he is at odds with the apocalyptists, and closer to Marxism.[40] Is it not possible to affirm both a historical hope and a transcendent hope?

b. Laws asks 'whether apocalyptic is really seriously interested in the created order in itself, or whether the elements of the cosmos are not rather seen as symbols for those spiritual forces whose activities give an added dimension to human affairs and ultimately determine their outcome.'[41] The tentative way in which Moltmann presents this point about apocalyptic's interest in the cosmos[42] suggests that he is not entirely convinced of it himself – though of course even if he were proved wrong about apocalyptic, that would not

---

[34] 'Introduction to the "Theology of Hope" ', in *The Experiment Hope* (Philadelphia, 1975), p. 49. [35] *Ibid.*, p. 51.

[36] It should be noted that Moltmann himself lists some of the dangers inherent in apocalypticism – see *Religion, Revolution and the Future* (New York, 1969), p. 218.

[37] *The Rediscovery of Apocalyptic*, p. 108. R. Alves speaks forcefully on the dangers of a utopian vision of the future which is quite unrelated to present circumstances, *A Theology of Human Hope* (Washington, 1969), p. 102.

[38] Above, pp. 37f. [39] See p. 94.

[40] Moltmann acknowledges the influence on him of the East German neo-Marxist Ernst Bloch and his book *Das Prinzip Hoffnung* (3 volumes, Frankfurt, 1959).

[41] *What about the New Testament?*, p. 93. [42] *Theology of Hope*, pp. 136f.

invalidate his belief that Christian hope concerns not only individuals but the whole world.

c. The stress on the 'openness' of the future fits uneasily with apocalyptic determinism. Admittedly, as we have seen above, the determinism is not so rigid as is commonly supposed.[43] But Moltmann is engaging in a dubious *tour de force* when he insists on the openness and the limitless possibilities of the future in the face of apocalyptic determinism.

Moltmann's theology does not depend on apocalyptic thought in such a crucial way as Pannenberg's. Even if his use of apocalyptic were totally invalid, it would leave no glaring holes in his argument for a 'theology of hope'. For his exposition of hope is based not so much on particular apocalyptic themes as on the biblical theme of 'promise' and on more general theological and philosophical considerations. Perhaps the chief importance of his scheme is that it opens up the possibility of real dialogue with Marxism about hope within history for mankind. But his concentration on historical hope to the apparent exclusion of hope beyond death surely gives too much away to Marxism. And it is difficult to determine precisely what he means when he uses terms like 'resurrection' and 'parousia'. Superficially, he may seem to understand them quite literally, but in the context of his thought as a whole that appears unlikely.

Carl E. Braaten

Even more than Moltmann, the American Carl Braaten uses apocalyptic in an allusive and provocative way rather than in a precise way. In numerous writings which use what he calls 'apocalyptic themes', he hardly ever refers to any particular text in apocalyptic literature. Yet his more symbolic, allusive use of apocalyptic may in some respects get closer to the 'atmosphere' of the apocalyptists than many more precise scholarly studies.[44]

Dependent to some extent on Pannenberg and Moltmann, Braaten

[43] Above, pp. 38f.

[44] I am not of course suggesting that Braaten is not a serious scholar; rather I am trying to describe the 'flavour' of his work. Good samples of his thought may be seen in *The Future of God* (New York, 1969) and *Christ and Counter-Christ: Apocalyptic Themes in Theology and Culture* (Philadelphia, 1972); more briefly in 'The Significance of Apocalypticism for Systematic Theology', *Interpretation* 25, 1971, pp. 480–499.

works out the implications of his conviction that 'the strength of a gospel is derived from the hopes it inspires in the hearts of men.'[45] He sees apocalyptic as a source of hope. His insights derive partly from his sympathy towards the mentality of the apocalyptists: they were people who saw society 'from the bottom up rather than from the top down'. Since Christianity still functions largely 'as the ideological tool of the ruling classes, perhaps nothing could be more useful than a renaissance of the apocalyptic vision born in the graveyards, the catacombs, at the bottom of society or outside the gate'.[46] And he knows that a Christianity which cannot compete with Marxism is useless: 'Christianity without eschatology and Marxism without transcendence are two heresies fighting each other.'[47] We may draw attention to three aspects of his use of apocalyptic.

a. For Braaten the essence of apocalypticism lies in one of its most despised features – its *dualism*.[48] Interpreted symbolically rather than literally, this means that history moves forward through the mediation of mutually antagonistic forces. Hence apocalyptic may offer support for a theology of liberation rather than of development or evolution.

b. The apocalyptic symbol of resurrection answers the quest for human fulfilment and a transcendent meaning to life.[49]

c. Apocalyptic's vision of freedom on a cosmic scale provokes systematic theology to work out its implications in an ecological concern for the whole earth, and a missionary concern for the movement towards one universal religion.[50]

These theses are expanded in Braaten's books and their implications for the church worked out. Where he follows Pannenberg or Moltmann closely, he is vulnerable to the same criticisms as they are. When he refers continually to the 'symbols' of apocalyptic one is left wondering how far the Jewish apocalyptists would have recog-

[45] *History and Hermeneutics* (London, 1968), p. 176.

[46] *Christ and Counter-Christ*, p. vii.

[47] *Ibid.*, p. 13.

[48] *Christ and Counter-Christ*, p. 8; *Interpretation* 25, p. 491. *Cf.* Moltmann's stress on 'radical discontinuity', above, pp. 56f. The 'Death of God' theologian Thomas Altizer makes rather similar use of apocalyptic dualism – see *The Gospel of Christian Atheism* (London, 1967), pp. 46–48, 82–84; and several of his essays in *Radical Theology and the Death of God*, written with William Hamilton (Harmondsworth, 1968).

[49] *Interpretation* 25, pp. 493–495; *Christ and Counter-Christ*, pp. 40–53.

[50] *Interpretation* 25, pp. 495–498. On the issue of 'universal religion', see below, pp. 124ff.

nized their own beliefs in his. But perhaps the chief value of his work is that he takes the more theoretical studies of his mentors and demonstrates in a creative and challenging way what *difference* such a future-orientation makes to the life of the church and the world.

Can apocalyptic be relevant?

In her article under this title, Laws is mostly critical of those who have made use of apocalyptic in their theologies. From a study of Mark 13 and Revelation she concludes that 'the apocalyptic mould broke in the hands of those who most tried to use it, and that they broke it deliberately because of their Christian presuppositions. And if that is so, then it must raise a doubt about the value of appealing to apocalyptic *per se* in subsequent Christian theology.'[51] This seems to me to be over-cautious if I was right in suggesting that the relation between New Testament Christianity and Jewish apocalyptic was not one of opposition but of decisive fulfilment.[52]

There are still many unanswered questions. There are historical questions about the background of the apocalyptists, about the differences between earlier and later apocalypses, about the relationships between Jewish apocalypses and similar pagan literature, about the extent of apocalyptic influence on early Christianity. There are theological questions, about the relationship of apocalyptic literature to the biblical canon, and about which features of apocalyptic thought are compatible with genuine Christianity and which must be discarded. But a truly Christian theology can hardly ignore *some* of the insights discovered by the apocalyptists – even if there remains disagreement about the particular insights highlighted by scholars such as Pannenberg, Moltmann and Braaten. The apocalyptists' conviction that the meaning of history can only be found beyond history, that human life can only find its true fulfilment in a transcendent future beyond death, and that all men stand subject to God's judgment, is not lightly to be set aside.[53] In the following three

---

[51] *What about the New Testament?* p. 101.
[52] Above, p. 49.
[53] *Cf.* H. H. Rowley's chapter on 'The Enduring Message of Apocalyptic' in *The Relevance of Apocalyptic* (London, [3]1963), pp. 166–192. For a more tentative approach see S. Laws, *What about the New Testament?* p. 101. I should add that, whilst I take this threefold conviction to be a fair way of summarizing some basic beliefs of the apocalyptists, our three modern theologians

chapters we shall study the particular *Christian* form which these convictions came to acquire.

---

would not necessarily express themselves in quite this way. Pannenberg, for example, as we have seen, speaks not of revelation or meaning *beyond* history but *in* history – though only in the *whole* of history as it can be viewed from the end. I have expressed doubt about whether Moltmann believes in life after death. And not many theologians have much to say about divine judgment as it has been traditionally understood.

Chapter Five

The future of Jesus Christ: the parousia

I have argued that apocalyptic thought forms an indispensable background to the Christian hope which emerges in the New Testament. And I have observed that the distinctive and unifying feature of *Christian* eschatology is its Christological orientation. Therefore we will now study the hope of Christ's coming again.

The 'second coming' of Christ features prominently enough in the traditional creeds of the Christian church, as well as in newspaper cartoons depicting sandwich-board men who are presumed to be out of touch with the real world. The doctrine is prominent, too, in the New Testament, being mentioned in almost every book. Strictly speaking, the New Testament does not use the term 'second coming' or 'return' of Christ (though Heb. 9:28 comes very close to it). It speaks rather of an 'arrival' or 'appearance' or 'revelation' of Christ in the future. But since the New Testament makes a clear distinction between Christ's having come already in humility and his future coming in glory, we are surely justified in using the traditional terminology of Christ's 'return' or 'second coming'. That is not meant to imply the absence of Christ in the interim, or to deny that in a real sense he 'comes' continually in judgment and blessing to men throughout history. Rather it emphasizes that whereas Christ's presence now is spiritual and invisible, his final coming will be public and visible, and he will bring this age to a close. He will pass judgment on the lives of men, and he will gather his people into God's final kingdom.

If this, in essence, is what the traditional teaching asserts, what do the theologians make of it? In the first place, they often use the word *parousia* as a theological technical term. It is one of the various Greek words by which the New Testament writers refer to this 'coming' of Christ.[1] *Parousia*, which in Greek conveys the ideas both of 'coming' and of 'presence', and in Hellenistic culture was used of the joyful ceremonial visit of a ruler to his subjects, refers to Christ's glorious coming in, for example, Matthew 24:3, 27, 37, 39; 1 Thessalonians 2:19; 4:15; 2 Thessalonians 2:1, 8; James 5:7f.; 2 Peter 3:4, 12. But there is no reason in principle why one of the other New Testament words, such as *epiphaneia* ('appearing') or *apokalypsis* ('revelation') should not have been adopted as the theologians' technical term rather than *parousia*.

Interpretations of the doctrine vary widely. There are some, mostly 'popular', writers who interpret the biblical teaching in a very literal way, never even pausing to consider whether the New Testament writers themselves expected to be taken quite so literally. The various parts of the Bible have then to be fitted together rather like the pieces of a jigsaw puzzle, on the assumption that when taken literally they will fit together somehow. This approach has led to conflict between conservative schools of thought over how the messages of different parts of Scripture are to be related to each other. In particular, different answers are given to the question whether the parousia will take place before or after the thousand year reign of Christ on earth mentioned in Revelation 20 ('premillennialism' and 'postmillennialism' respectively). One particular brand of premillennialism, known as dispensationalism, has been very influential during the last hundred years among evangelicals, especially in America.[2]

Some other conservative scholars offer a restatement of the traditional doctrine, but are more sensitive to the issues involved in biblical criticism and to the problem of literal versus symbolic interpretation. Some of these writers who have made significant contributions are G. C. Berkouwer, *The Return of Christ* (Grand Rapids, 1972); G. E. Ladd, *Jesus and the Kingdom* (London, 1964; revised edition entitled *The Presence of the Future*, Grand Rapids, 1974); A. L. Moore, *The Parousia in the New Testament* (Leiden,

---

[1] For a discussion of the term and its background, see *TDNT* 5, pp. 858–871; E. Best, *The First and Second Epistles to the Thessalonians* (London, 1972), pp. 347–354.

[2] There is a scathing treatment of dispensationalism, and other brands of millennialism, in J. Barr, *Fundamentalism* (London, 1977), pp. 190–207. For a more irenical approach see J. R. Ross, 'Evangelical Alternatives', in C. E. Armerding and W. W. Gasque (eds.), *Dreams, Visions and Oracles* (Grand Rapids, 1977), pp. 117–129. I have discussed these approaches to eschatology in *I Believe in the Second Coming of Christ* (London, forthcoming).

1966); H. Ridderbos, *The Coming of the Kingdom* (ET, Philadelphia, 1962); R. Schnackenburg, *God's Rule and Kingdom* (ET, London, 1963). In this chapter, however, I shall not discuss these writings in detail, but shall try to evaluate the four major treatments of the parousia which have been influential in recent years.[3]

Rudolf Bultmann and 'demythologizing'

R. Bultmann accepted Schweitzer's conclusion that Jesus expected an imminent inbreaking of the kingdom of God. But his 'demythologizing' of the New Testament's eschatology led him to a very distinctive and very influential understanding of it. His viewpoint is summarized in his famous article 'New Testament and Mythology',[4] though his 'demythologizing' approach to the New Testament is evident in much earlier writing.[5] The New Testament, according to Bultmann, is full of mythology. But what does he mean by 'myth'? He defines myth in at least three ways – which may not be entirely consistent with each other.[6] Firstly, he says, 'Mythology is the use of imagery to express the other worldly in terms of this world and the divine in terms of human life, the other side in terms of this side. For instance, divine transcendence is expressed as spatial distance.'[7]

In addition to that explicit definition, Bultmann also refers to the

---

[3] There is not space to discuss everyone who deserves mention. For a brief evaluation of some other theologians, see A. C. Thiselton, 'The Parousia in Modern Theology: Some Questions and Comments', *TynB* 27, 1976, pp. 27–53. And for a thorough survey of all the main viewpoints on Jesus' eschatological message, see N. Perrin, *The Kingdom of God in the Teaching of Jesus* (London, 1963). A wide-ranging survey of modern interpretations of New Testament eschatology is by C. Brown in C. Brown (ed.), *The New International Dictionary of New Testament Theology*, 2 (Exeter, 1976), pp. 901–931. But NB also that numerous modern theologians, *e.g.* Moltmann and Pannenberg, write much about the future whilst saying very little about the parousia. I have expressed my own understanding of the parousia in *I Believe in the Second Coming of Christ*, and briefly at the end of this chapter.

[4] In *Kerygma and Myth*, 1, ed. H.-W. Bartsch (ET, London, 1953), pp. 1–44. In this and a series of subsequent volumes Bultmann's standpoint and various critical reactions to him may be found. A fuller introduction to Bultmann's thought is his *Jesus Christ and Mythology* (New York, 1958). See also the sympathetic critique in J. Macquarrie, *The Scope of Demythologizing* (London, 1960); and the more critical article by P. S. Minear, 'Rudolf Bultmann's Interpretation of New Testament Eschatology', in C. W. Kegley (ed.), *The Theology of Rudolf Bultmann* (London, 1966), pp. 65–82.

[5] *E.g.*, in *Jesus and the Word* (1926, ET, London, [2]1958).

[6] See A. C. Thiselton, 'The Parousia in Modern Theology', *TynB* 27, 1976, p. 35, n. 22.

[7] *Kerygma and Myth*, 1, p. 10, n. 2. *Cf. Jesus Christ and Mythology*, pp. 19–21.

mythical world-view according to which God intervenes in human affairs from time to time, and Christ will soon come on the clouds of heaven to complete the work of redemption.[8] This implies a definition of 'mythological' in terms of supernatural events, or acts of God 'from above'.

Thirdly, Bultmann stresses that myth *objectifies* the reality to which it refers; *i.e.*, it speaks as though God were an object, as though his activity consisted of objective acts within space and time which could be investigated by historical science. 'Mythological thinking . . . naïvely objectifies the beyond as though it were something within the world.' 'The real purpose of myth is not to present an objective picture of the world as it is, but to express man's understanding of himself in the world in which he lives. . . . But that purpose is impeded and obscured by the terms in which it is expressed.'[9] For example, the myth of the coming of the Son of man on the clouds of heaven looks like a description of an actual event in the future, whereas its real purpose is to express the message that Christ 'comes to me'. This mythological language should therefore be 'demythologized', or translated into language which better expresses the underlying 'personal' meaning of the myth. And Bultmann insists that demythologizing does not mean simply stripping away the myth as though it were irrelevant, but *interpreting* it.[10] We shall see in a moment what form Bultmann's interpretation takes.

Apart from his view of the nature and function of myth, Bultmann justifies demythologizing on four further grounds. First, the modern scientific world-view makes the primitive Christian myths incredible. 'The kerygma is incredible to modern man, for he is convinced that the mythical view of the world is obsolete. . . . We can no longer look for the return of the Son of Man on the clouds of heaven or hope that the faithful will meet him in the air (1 Thes. 4:15ff.).'[11]

Secondly, 'the mythical eschatology is untenable for the simple reason that the parousia of Christ never took place as the New

---

[8] *Kerygma and Myth*, 1, pp. 1f.

[9] 'On the Problem of Demythologizing', in *New Testament Issues*, ed. R. Batey (London, 1970), p. 41; *Kerygma and Myth*, 1, pp. 10f.

[10] See *Jesus Christ and Mythology*, pp. 18, 45.

[11] *Kerygma and Myth*, 1, pp. 3f. *Cf. ibid:* 'It is impossible to use electric light and the wireless and to avail ourselves of modern medical and surgical discoveries, and at the same time to believe in the New Testament world of spirits and miracles.'

Testament expected. History did not come to an end, and, as every schoolboy knows, it will continue to run its course.'[12]

Thirdly, modern man's understanding of himself invites demythologizing of the New Testament's message. Men today do not think of themselves as exposed to interference by external powers. So, for example, they find New Testament teaching about the Holy Spirit and the sacraments incomprehensible.[13]

Fourthly, the New Testament itself invites demythologizing. Many of its mythological features are mutually contradictory. For example, Jesus is sometimes represented as Messiah, sometimes as the Second Adam; the doctrine of creation is incompatible with the conception of the 'rulers of this world' (1 Cor. 2:6ff.). A particular contradiction running through the New Testament is the contradiction between statements that human life is determined by cosmic forces, and statements that we are challenged to decision. Demythologizing will remove the contradiction. Moreover, demythologizing is already practised by New Testament writers themselves, especially by Paul and John, as we shall see in a moment.

Now if the biblical myths are to be interpreted, *how* should they be interpreted? What is the underlying truth of the myths which can provide the key to correct interpretation? Bultmann's claim is that the true meaning of the myths lies in their understanding of human existence: they must be interpreted existentially. 'Myth should be interpreted not cosmologically, but anthropologically, or better still, existentially.'[14] Influenced by the earlier Barth and by the existentialist philosopher Heidegger, Bultmann found his interpretative key in existentialist philosophy. He justifies this approach by arguing that both existentialism and the Bible are concerned about human existence.[15] (He does not, however, imagine that existentialist philosophy and the Bible are saying the same thing: he would argue that existentialism focuses the *problem* of man's existence and the need for 'authentic existence', whereas the Christian message gives man the *power* to make the decisive choice for authenticity.)

Thus, according to Bultmann, even though Paul retained belief in a future parousia, resurrection and judgment, his message that the turning-point from the old world to the new has already taken place

[12] *Ibid.*, p. 5.   [13] *Ibid.*, p. 6.   [14] *Ibid.*, p. 10.
[15] *Ibid.*, p. 12; *Jesus Christ and Mythology*, pp. 45–59.

in Christ represents a partial demythologizing of primitive eschatology. Paul's major concern is with the present existence of the believer. 'In Paul . . . eschatology has wholly lost its sense as goal of history and is in fact understood as the goal of the individual human being.'[16] Demythologizing took a more radical turn in John's Gospel, which eliminates altogether futurist eschatology and concentrates on the present life of the individual believer.[17]

This way of understanding the New Testament's eschatological message leads to the following characteristic emphases in Bultmann's thought.

a. Jesus Christ is the eschatological event, by which God has brought an end to the old world. For the believer, therefore, who is 'a new creature in Christ', the old world has already reached its end.[18]

b. Whereas the present time is all-important, any notion of a truly futurist eschatology is minimized. 'I do not identify the present *tout court* with the eschaton, . . . but I do assert with the New Testament that we are confronted with the eschaton in the Now of encounter.' 'I do not see why it is necessary to think of a temporal end of time.'[19]

c. History is interpreted in individualistic terms. Meaning in history is not to be found in the causal connection of events, but in the life of the individual as he responds to situations and to God. 'The meaning of history lies always in the present, and when the present is conceived as the eschatological present by the Christian faith the meaning in history is realized.' To the man who claims to see no meaning in history, the Christian faith says he should look not at universal history but into his own personal history: 'In every moment slumbers the possibility of being the eschatological moment. You must awaken it.'[20]

[16] 'History and Eschatology in the New Testament', *NTS* 1, 1954, p. 13. A similar assertion about Jesus' eschatological teaching is made in *Theology of the New Testament*, 1 (ET, London, 1952), p. 23.

[17] Cf. *Jesus Christ and Mythology*, p. 33. This judgment of course involves Bultmann in attributing to a later editor passages such as Jn. 5:28f., 6:40, where a futurist eschatology is found. See his *The Gospel of John* (ET, Oxford, 1971).

[18] *History and Eschatology* (Edinburgh, 1957), p. 151.

[19] 'A Reply to the Theses of J. Schniewind', *Kerygma and Myth*, 1, pp. 116, 118. Cf. the discussion in N. Q. Hamilton, *The Holy Spirit and Eschatology in Paul* (Edinburgh-London, 1957), pp. 78f.

[20] *History and Eschatology*, p. 155. Cf. the whole book, *e.g.*, pp. 43, 47–49, 109, 120–122, 139–155.

d. The New Testament's eschatological language is constantly interpreted in terms of individual existence. For example, in a discussion of 'Man Between the Times according to the New Testament', Bultmann interprets the teaching of Paul and John that the new age has already begun. The existential meaning of this, he says, is that *my* past as a sinner has been replaced by a freedom for *my* future. The man who surrenders himself to God is free from anxiety *(Angst)*, 'free from himself as he actually is as he comes out of his past'.[21] 'My restatement of it (the New Testament's eschatology) demonstrates the character of faith as freedom for the future.'[22] The word 'eschatological' has lost its temporal meaning, and is synonymous with 'involving man's true relationship with God', and 'a life based on invisible, intangible realities'.[23] 'Eschatological existence' means being 'a new creature' (2 Cor. 5:17).[24]

e. Eschatological language refers to the crisis of decision in which men stand as they are confronted by the kerygma. 'The eschatological message of Jesus . . . can be understood only when one considers the conception of man which in the last analysis underlies it.' The underlying conviction is that 'even in the present man stands in the crisis of decision, that the present is for him the last hour.'[25] Minear summarizes the point in this way: 'The radical dualism between the two ages was simply the occasion for grasping the absoluteness of man's choice: either the world or God's reign.'[26]

f. God's purposes for the future can be spoken of only with great reserve. Although Jesus himself shared his contemporaries' expectation of a great eschatological drama, he refrained from depicting the details of heaven and hell; he refused to calculate the time of the end.[27] Similarly 'the Christian hope knows *that* it hopes, but it does not know what it hopes for.'[28] In face of death the Christian can hope not because he is assured of resurrection in a specific and desirable form – 'for all pictures of a glory after death can only be

[21] *Existence and Faith* (ET, London, 1961), pp. 254f. See further pp. 255–266 on 'openness to the future'.
[22] 'Bultmann Replies to his Critics', *Kerygma and Myth*, 1, p. 205.
[23] *The Gospel of John,*, pp. 481, 483, 485; *Kerygma and Myth*, 1, p. 113.
[24] *Kerygma and Myth*, 1, p. 20.   [25] *Jesus and the Word*, p. 47.
[26] *The Theology of Rudolf Bultmann*, p. 71.   [27] *Jesus and the Word*, pp. 35f.
[28] Bultmann in G. Bornkamm, R. Bultmann, F. K. Schumann *Die christliche Hoffnung und das Problem der Entmythologisierung* (Stuttgart, 1954), p. 58, quoted in G. O'Collins, *Man and His New Hopes* (New York, 1969), p. 58.

the wishful images of imagination' – but simply because 'for him who is open to all that is future as the future of the coming God, death has lost its terror'.[29]

Underlying this interpretation of the New Testament's eschatological language is Bultmann's fundamental conviction of the wrongness of any language which objectifies God.[30] As J. D. G. Dunn stresses, the real problem for Bultmann is not the problem of mythological language as such, but the problem of any language which objectifies God. And demythologizing is possible only in terms of existentialist interpretation because 'only the language of existential encounter enables Bultmann to speak of God's activity without objectifying it.'[31] Hence his rejection of any temporally future cosmological eschatology. According to Minear's summary of Bultmann's thought, an eschatology which concerns itself with the future of the cosmos is *per se* mythological because 'it inevitably confuses history with nature and reduces human existence to the realm of cosmic objectivity.'[32]

Among the merits of Bultmann's approach is his reminder that language about the parousia is not intended merely to satisfy curiosity about the future, but rather to influence actions and attitudes in the present time. But his scheme also involves serious inadequacies. Critics have drawn attention to the following points, amongst others.

a. Bultmann's use of the term 'myth' is often imprecise. His basic definition (above, p. 65 and n. 4) is too all-embracing, allowing no distinction to be made between myth, analogy and metaphor. If valid, this definition would make myth indispensable to any talk about God.[33] Later he argued that it is sometimes legitimate to speak of God and his activity by analogy (*i.e.*, without objectifying him).[34]

[29] 'The Christian Hope and the Problem of Demythologizing', *ExpT* 65, 1953–54, p. 278. *Cf.* G. O'Collins, *Man and His New Hopes*, pp. 62f.   [30] See above, p. 66.

[31] 'Demythologizing – the Problem of Myth in the New Testament', in *New Testament Interpretation*, ed. I. H. Marshall (Exeter, 1977), pp. 296f. and notes. Bultmann nevertheless resists the idea of completely demythologizing God and his activity. He wishes to preserve – illogically? – the New Testament kerygma's proclamation of 'a decisive act of God in Christ'. See *Jesus Christ and Mythology*, pp. 60ff.; and the discussion in J. Macquarrie, *The Scope of Demythologizing*, e.g., pp. 11–13, 244.

[32] *The Theology of Rudolf Bultmann*, p. 66.

[33] See H. Thielicke, *The Evangelical Faith*, 1 (ET, Grand Rapids, 1974), pp. 66–114.

[34] *Kerygma and Myth*, 1, pp. 196f.

But once this is acknowledged, the question immediately arises: how much of the New Testament's 'mythological language' is in fact metaphor, analogy or symbol, consciously selected by the writers, and therefore not merely the result of primitive and unthinking conceptualization as Bultmann supposes? And if we are dealing with metaphors, analogies and symbols deliberately chosen by the authors, can Bultmann be so sure that his demythologizing interpretation does not destroy the authors' intended meaning?[35]

b. Bultmann's claim that his demythologizing programme follows the example set by the New Testament writers themselves goes beyond the evidence. Would Paul have agreed that his 'real intention' is being carried out in Bultmann's reduction of the temporally future parousia to 'the goal of the individual human being'? Far from it. Paul's apocalyptic language in 1 Corinthians 15 seems specifically chosen in order to assert that there remains a future fulfilment to God's purposes – in contrast to the individualizing and spiritualizing concepts of Hellenistic 'enthusiasts'. And even though John 'demythologizes' apocalyptic concepts in the direction of a more 'realized' eschatology, he does not abandon futurist eschatology.[36] If demythologizing by the New Testament authors themselves is to be taken as a justification and as a norm for our demythologizing, is there not a case for saying that our demythologizing should not go beyond theirs?

c. Bultmann's concept of 'modernity' is open to criticism. According to Macquarrie, he seems sometimes to be trying 'not only to interpret the gospel in terms of the modern world-picture (which is legitimate), but also to present it in relation to the modern secularized self-understanding'. But 'if the modern self-understanding is secularized, it can never understand anything to be an act of God'.[37] Bultmann's dismissal of the idea of divine interventions in history as being the mythological formulations of a pre-scientific age is particularly unfortunate. W. Pannenberg comments: 'The acceptance of

[35] See the discussion in J. D. G. Dunn, *New Testament Interpretation*, pp. 296f.; J. Macquarrie, *The Scope of Demythologizing*, pp. 198–216; D. S. Cairns, *A Gospel Without Myth? Bultmann's Challenge to the Preacher* (London, 1960), pp. 85f., 89–93, 196.

[36] O. Cullmann shows that even without the texts which Bultmann attributes to a later editor, John's eschatology still retains a future aspect; see *Salvation in History* (ET, London, 1967), pp. 289–291.

[37] *The Scope of Demythologizing*, p. 232; see also pp. 229–233, 236.

divine intervention in the course of events . . . is fundamental to every religious understanding of the world, including one which is not mythical in the sense in which comparative religion uses the term.' And he adds that 'the eschatological conceptions of apocalyptic which are important in the New Testament cannot be understood as mythical without qualification'.[38] So the notion of divine involvement in history – with the parousia as the final, decisive intervention of God – is not to be rejected because it arose in a pre-scientific age. The real problem is not this supposed mythology, but Bultmann's conception of an apparently 'closed', mechanistic universe from which divine intervention is excluded *a priori*.

d. Bultmann's critique of cosmic eschatology may be criticized in its turn. Do we have to accept his sharp distinction between nature (the world, man's environment) and history (the range of possibilities for the individual, requiring his decision)? Why is eschatological language appropriate only with reference to this personal history? He argues that a cosmological eschatology would reduce man's responsibility for the world and its future.[39] But this seems strangely misguided in view of the way in which various 'theologies of hope' have used a cosmological eschatology as a basis for responsible involvement in social and political issues. Bultmann's approach, by contrast, is far too individualistic.[40]

e. To exchange the future orientation of eschatology for an existential interpretation is to distort the Christian message. This has been the frequent complaint of O. Cullmann and W. G. Kümmel, whom we shall study below.[41] For, however much it is right to stress the relevance of the kerygma to personal experience, the Christian faith must also say something about Jesus as *Jesus*, about *his* past and *his* future. It is Bultmann's implicit assumption that New Testament eschatology is to be interpreted *only* in existential terms which threatens all meaningful continuity with original Christ-

[38] 'The Later Dimensions of Myth in Biblical and Christian Tradition', in *Basic Questions in Theology*, 3, (ET, London, 1973), pp. 14, 67.

[39] 'Reply', in *The Theology of Rudolf Bultmann*, ed. C. W. Kegley, pp. 267f.

[40] See O'Collins, *Man and His New Hopes*, pp. 59–61; P. S. Minear, *The Theology of Rudolf Bultmann*, pp. 76–82. Bultmann's 'Reply' may have blunted some of Minear's criticisms, but has certainly not refuted them.

[41] *Cf*. K. Rahner, 'The Hermeneutics of Eschatological Assertions', in *Theological Investigations*, 4 (ET, London, 1966), p. 326.

ianity.[42] Thiselton puts the issue like this: 'To say "Christ will come; live accordingly", is to say *more* than merely "Live *as if* Christ were to come".'[43] To say 'live responsibly, because there is a final judgment', is to say *more* than 'live responsibly'. To say 'Christ must reign until he has put all his enemies under his feet' (1 Cor. 15:25), is to say *more* than 'Christ is Lord of *my* life.'

f. Indeed, it is difficult to see how a 'myth' or doctrine can have significance for personal existence unless there is some objective truth in it. K. Löwith asserts: 'Both Heidegger and Bultmann insist that the "true" futurity of the human and divine *eschaton*, respectively, lies in the instant of our decision. They ignore the fact that neither death nor the Kingdom of God could ever provoke a decision, and even less a radical change in man's conduct and attitude, unless they were expected as real events in the future.'[44]

Bultmann's approach, then, is an extremely significant attempt to tackle the problems created by the New Testament's use of 'myth', symbol and analogy. We should welcome his insistence that the doctrine of the parousia should be interpreted in a way which highlights its relevance to the present time. But his obsession with the problem of objectifying God causes him to demythologize much of the New Testament message that cannot be demythologized because it is saying something basic to the Christian message which can only be said in the language of 'myth', symbol or analogy. In particular, his elimination of the parousia as a future, decisive event at the end of history removes something which is of the essence of the New Testament's message. It is a message both about personal decision and responsibility, and about Christ's coming and final judgment.

C. H. Dodd and 'realized eschatology'

Futurist eschatology was called in question for different reasons by the British scholar C. H. Dodd. In an article published in 1934 he argued that Paul's eschatology developed away from the Jewish

[42] *Cf.* J. D. G. Dunn, *New Testament Interpretation*, pp. 295f., 299.
[43] *TynB* 27, 1976, pp. 39f.
[44] *Meaning in History* (Chicago, 1949), p. 253, n. 21. *Cf.* D. S. Cairns, *A Gospel Without Myth?* pp. 151f.; H. Ott, 'Rudolf Bultmann's Philosophy of History', in C. W. Kegley, *The Theology of Rudolf Bultmann*, p. 58.

apocalyptic scheme which determined his early thought as a Christian.[45] 'His picture of the end in 2 Thessalonians is painted in colours from the crudest palette of Jewish eschatology.'[46] But gradually this futurist, world-denying eschatology, with its emphasis on an imminent parousia, was replaced by a world-accepting approach which emphasized the present rule of Christ over all things.

In the following year Dodd's book *The Parables of the Kingdom* introduced the term 'realized eschatology'.[47] He thus drew attention – partly in reaction against Schweitzer – to those passages in the Gospels, and particularly in the parables, where Jesus seems to affirm that the kingdom of God is *already present* through his ministry. For Dodd, the heart of Jesus' message was that because of his coming the eschaton was no longer merely future but present; it had moved from the sphere of expectation to the sphere of experience.

His emphasis on 'realized eschatology' rests on two main arguments. First, there are certain sayings of Jesus which clearly proclaim the kingdom of God as a matter of present experience during his ministry: Matthew 11:2–11 (= Lk. 7:18–30); Matthew 11:12 (= Lk. 16:16); Matthew 12:28 (= Lk. 11:20); Mark 1:14f.; Luke 10:23f. (= Mt. 13:16f.); Luke 11:31f. (= Mt. 12:41f.).[48] Such passages indicate 'the impact upon this world of the "powers of the age to come" in a series of events, unprecedented and unrepeatable, now in actual process.'[49] Even Mark 1:15 (RSV, 'the kingdom of God is at hand') does not refer to the imminence of the kingdom but to its presence: underlying the Greek *ēngiken* is an Aramaic word meaning 'has arrived'.[50]

Secondly, Dodd offers a radical reinterpretation of many parables of Jesus. For example, parables such as the Tares (Mt. 13:24–30) and the Dragnet (Mt. 13:47–50) have traditionally been interpreted with reference to the final judgment at the parousia. But according to Dodd the Tares teaches that the presence of sinners in Israel is no sign that the kingdom of God is delayed; and the Dragnet is an exhortation to fishers of men to cast their net widely.[51] Moreover,

---

[45] 'The Mind of Paul: II', reprinted in *New Testament Studies* (Manchester, 1953), pp. 83–128.
[46] *Ibid.*, p. 121.
[47] See the third edition (London, 1936), pp. 50f., 198.
[48] *Ibid.*, pp. 43–48.   [49] *Ibid.*, p. 51.
[50] *Ibid.*, pp. 44f.   [51] *Ibid.*, pp. 183–185; 187–189.

it was the early church and the evangelists themselves who began this process of taking parables of Jesus which originally referred to the presence of the kingdom and the challenge provoked by Jesus' ministry, and re-applying them to a future coming of the kingdom and a future judgment. So, for example, Matthew has found in the parable of the Dragnet 'an allegory of the last judgment', which 'is clearly secondary and may be ignored.'[52] The parable of the Ten Virgins has been turned into a parable about the parousia by the addition of certain allegorical features which must be removed if Jesus' original meaning is to be discerned.[53]

Thus Dodd argues that in Jesus' teaching the emphasis falls on the presence of the kingdom in his own person and ministry. Jesus did have expectations for the future, which were threefold: his own impending death; disaster for the Jewish people; his own survival of death and the vindication of God's plan in his own person.[54] But he did not expect the parousia: it was the early church who took his predictions of vindication and expressed some of them as forecasts of his resurrection and others as forecasts of a future apocalyptic 'coming on the clouds'.[55] Christians learned to hope for the parousia as the final event in a chronological series, and thus fell back into the apocalypticism from which Jesus had sought to break free. Dodd does not deny that Jesus used apocalyptic language, but believes that he understood such language in a highly symbolic way: it expresses eternal truths and unfolds the meaning of Jesus' coming in Galilee and Jerusalem, rather than predicting a distinct, future coming.[56] An accurate reflection of Jesus' eschatological teaching is therefore found in the 'developed' eschatology of Paul's later letters, and in the distinctly 'realized' eschatology of John's Gospel.[57]

---

[52] Ibid., p. 187.

[53] Ibid., pp. 171–174. It is important to read The Parables of the Kingdom, especially chapters 5 and 6, to see how Dodd carries through his attempt to get behind the Gospels to a hypothetical 'original' version of the parables. His method and conclusions had much influence on the later work of J. Jeremias, The Parables of Jesus (ET, London, revised edition 1963).

[54] See The Parables of the Kingdom, pp. 53–110.

[55] Ibid., pp. 98, 101.

[56] Ibid., pp. 105–110. For a discussion of Dodd's critical handling of apocalyptic, see N. Q. Hamilton, The Holy Spirit and Eschatology in Paul, pp. 56–60.

[57] On Paul, see the article referred to above, n. 45; on John, see The Interpretation of the Fourth Gospel (Cambridge, 1953), e.g., pp. 403–406; on both, see The Apostolic Preaching and its Developments (London, [2]1944), pp. 57–78.

In a talk broadcast in 1950 Dodd hinted at a significant modification of his view when he spoke of 'the final coming of the Son of man' as 'not an event *in* history' but as 'the point at which *all* history is taken up into the larger whole of God's eternal purpose'.[58] This seems to suggest a more explicit parousia doctrine than is found in Dodd's earlier work. But it is not developed, and his overwhelming emphasis remained on 'realized eschatology'.

The philosophical roots of Dodd's approach to eschatology are expounded in his *History and the Gospel* (London, 1938). He views history as the incomplete striving of this world towards the transcendent absolutes of the eternal world. The coming of Jesus to introduce the kingdom of God and to reveal the Absolute within history provided a purpose for all later history, rendering superfluous any other 'coming' or future goal.

One may discern here a preference for a metaphysical (Platonic) tension between this world and the eternal world, rather than for the temporal (biblical) tension between the 'already' and the 'not yet'. Hamilton suggests that Dodd's concern to make the gospel relevant made him suspicious of futurist and apocalyptic eschatology: futurist eschatology with its not-yet-realized benefits raises rather than solves the problem of relevance.[59] Another apologetic motive behind Dodd's thesis is that it enabled him to regard the New Testament's imminent expectation of the parousia as mistaken, without attributing that mistake to Jesus himself.

Dodd's 'realized eschatology' has been very influential in Britain, but has not met with general acceptance elsewhere. Its great merit is that it focuses attention on what surely is central in the New Testament: that God acted supremely and uniquely in Jesus Christ, that salvation is available through Christ, and that salvation is available now. But in order to highlight this message, he minimized or eliminated – by critical procedures which need to be questioned – the futurist eschatology of the Gospels. Criticisms such as the following have been made against him.[60]

[58] *The Coming of Christ* (Cambridge, 1951), p. 27. *Cf. The Founder of Christianity* (London, 1971), pp. 115–118.
[59] Hamilton, *The Holy Spirit and Eschatology in Paul*, pp. 54–56.
[60] An excellent survey and critique – including treatment of Dodd's controversial interpretation of Mark 9:1 (not discussed here on grounds of space) – may be found in N. Perrin, *The Kingdom of God in the Teaching of Jesus* (London, 1963), pp. 58–78.

a. Not all Dodd's 'clear passages' support his thesis as unambiguously as he suggests. Some critics have claimed that only by special pleading from a few Septuagint passages and by hypothetical reconstruction of Jesus' original Aramaic can *ēngiken* in Mark 1:15 (*cf.* Mt. 10:7) be translated 'has come'; the evangelists used the verb *engizein* in all other passages in the sense of 'drawing near'.[61] However, it must also be pointed out that several scholars, including some who are not sympathetic to Dodd's basic position, agree with him that Mark 1:15 and similar passages indicate the presence of the kingdom in Jesus.[62] A. L. Moore perhaps gets the balance right when he says that the passages listed by Dodd as indicating the presence of God's kingdom during Jesus' ministry (see above, p. 74) do indeed suggest a 'realized eschatology'; but it is still 'hidden and ambiguous, pointing forward to a yet future fulfilment of the old expectation of a manifest, universal, unequivocal presence'.[63] If so, Dodd is not justified in playing up 'realized eschatology' at the expense of 'futurist eschatology'.

b. The claim that allusions to the parousia in the Gospel parables derive not from Jesus but from his early followers and the evangelists themselves is arbitrary, and relies on unconvincing arguments. For example, Dodd's resolute removal of 'allegorical features' from the parable of the Ten Virgins reduces it to the level of general truths: a colourful warning against exclusion at the parousia is turned by him into an unspecific warning against coming catastrophe within history. But why the allegorical features should be removed is not explained, except that their removal brings the parable into line with the 'realized eschatology' already discerned in other passages. Similarly, there seems to be no reason why the parables of the Tares and the Dragnet should be interpreted as Dodd suggests – unless one has already decided that allusions to a future parousia and judgment are suspect.[64]

---

[61] See J. Y. Campbell, ' "The Kingdom of God has come" ', *ExpT* 48, 1936–37, pp. 91–94; W. G. Kümmel, *Promise and Fulfilment* (ET, London, 1957), pp. 22–25.

[62] G. E. Ladd, The Presence of the Future (Grand Rapids, 1974), pp. 110f.; I. H. Marshall, *The Gospel of Luke* (Exeter, 1978), p. 422.

[63] *The Parousia in the New Testament* (Leiden, 1966), pp. 56–58.

[64] For some further criticism of Dodd's handling of the parables, see A. L. Moore, *The Parousia in the New Testament*, pp. 64–66; W. G. Kümmel, *Promise and Fulfilment*, pp. 56–59, 132–138, etc.; I. H. Marshall, *Eschatology and the Parables* (London, 1963), esp. pp. 26–47.

   c. The importance of futurist eschatology for Paul and even for John cannot be minimized as readily as Dodd imagines. For Paul certainly, and probably for John, there is an essential tension between present and future, between 'already' and 'not yet'. To destroy that tension is seriously to distort their message.[65]

   d. Dodd's 'demythologizing' of futurist and apocalyptic eschatological language provokes critical questions. Why is the Platonic scheme which he favours more satisfactory than the Bible's own scheme, whereby God's purpose moves forward in time towards its consummation at the parousia? Why can he apparently envisage no half-way house between 'strict literalness' and a 'strictly symbolic' interpretation of apocalyptic concepts which eliminates the parousia as a genuinely future event?[66] Is it not possible and preferable to take seriously the element of imagery and symbol in biblical language without abandoning the biblical time-scheme, with its hope of a future parousia? Théo Preiss argued that since the Bible did not radically modify the spatial aspect of ancient cosmology – the 'above', the 'below', the underworld, *etc.* – we may readily demythologize these spatial ideas; but since the Bible changed fundamentally the *temporal* aspect of ancient cosmology, we dare not demythologize the Bible's temporal framework – unless we wish to promulgate a 'Christianity' significantly different from the Christianity of the New Testament.[67]

   'Realized eschatology', therefore, rightly emphasizes that according to the New Testament the kingdom of God was already present during the ministry of Jesus and is not merely an object of future hope. But, as Moore asserts, 'this "realisation" is connected in the New Testament directly with the person and work of Christ and therefore with the lowliness and hiddenness characteristic of his ministry. It therefore carries the promise of future fulfilment, indeed demands future fulfilment. . . . The present is evaluated falsely if it is seen only in the light of the past event (Incarnation) and not also

---

   [65] On this tension see the comments on Cullmann and Kümmel below, pp. 86f. For a critique of Dodd's treatment of Paul on this issue see N. Q. Hamilton, *The Holy Spirit and Eschatology in Paul*, pp. 61–70; and for brief comments on his understanding of Paul and John, see A. L. Moore, *The Parousia in the New Testament*, pp. 61–63.

   [66] See his discussion of apocalyptic in *The Parables of the Kingdom*, pp. 105–110, esp. pp. 106, 108.   [67] *Life in Christ* (ET, London, 1954), pp. 65f.

in the light of the future End. . . . The future for which Realised Eschatology looks misses entirely the historical particularity of the Parousia in the New Testament, a particularity which is strictly parallel to that attaching to the Incarnation' (*cf.* Acts 1:11).[68]

J. A. T. Robinson and 'inaugurated eschatology'

Another British scholar, John Robinson, himself much influenced by C. H. Dodd as well as by T. F. Glasson's book *The Second Advent* (London, third edition 1963), has written *Jesus and his Coming* (London, 1957).[69] This is a provocative and persuasive book, arguing that the parousia hope was not part of Jesus' expectation, but was an invention of the early church, sometime between AD 30 and 50. Jesus shared the contemporary Jewish expectation of the final vindication of God and his saints, an end to the present world-order, and final judgment and resurrection, and even saw himself as intimately connected with the final day. Yet that does not necessarily presuppose that he expected to 'come again' as the later New Testament writings and church tradition have taught.[70] Rather, Jesus used the familiar apocalyptic categories of vindication and *visitation*. He expected immediate vindication following from his sufferings, and this was fulfilled in his resurrection and going *to* God.[71] And the visitation of God took place mainly in his own ministry and its immediate consequences, including the fall of Jerusalem in AD 70.[72] In the Gospels explicit references to a parousia after an interval are 'a purely editorial feature'. Jesus did talk about 'the coming of the Son of man', but by this he meant 'the visitation of God to his people focused in the challenge and climax of his own ministry.'[73]

Robinson argues in a similar way to Dodd that the parables of crisis, which were used by Jesus to define the crisis created by his ministry, were re-applied by the early church and the evangelists to the future crisis of parousia and final judgment.[74]

But how does he deal with a passage such as Mark 14:62, where

---

[68] *The Parousia in the New Testament*, pp. 63f.

[69] The second edition (1979) is unchanged except for minor corrections and a two page preface giving cross-references to Robinson's book *Redating the New Testament* (London, 1976).

[70] *Jesus and his Coming*, pp. 36–39.   [71] *Ibid.*, pp. 39–58.

[72] *Ibid.*, pp. 59–82   [73] *Ibid.*, pp. 138, 141.   [74] *Ibid.*, pp. 64–72.

Jesus says: 'You will see the Son of man sitting at the right hand of Power, and coming with the clouds of heaven' (cf. Mt. 26:64; Lk. 22:69)? He sees here an allusion to Psalm 110:1, which speaks of divine vindication; and to Daniel 7:13, which speaks not of a coming *from* God, but of 'a coming *to* God in ascent and vindication'. So the two halves of Jesus' statement do not refer to two chronologically separate events – his resurrection and parousia – but are parallel statements both referring to the 'immediate vindication of himself and his cause, out of the very jaws of humiliation and defeat.'[75] It refers, then, to Jesus' resurrection and ensuing Lordship, not to his parousia.[76]

There is no parousia-expectation, according to Robinson, in the earliest strata of apostolic Christianity. The Aramaic prayer 'Marana tha' ('Our Lord, come', 1 Cor. 16:22) *need* be no more than a prayer that Christ be present, spiritually, at the eucharist (cf. Rev. 3:20).[77] And Acts 10:42, whilst announcing future judgment, does not state that judgment will take place only at some second coming.[78] The earliest clear evidence of belief in the parousia is in 1 and 2 Thessalonians, about AD 50.

Robinson believes that the hope of Christ's coming again arose from 'an unresolved crisis in the Christology of the primitive Church, centring in the problem whether or not the messianic event had yet taken place, whether *the Christ* had come or not. The solution, as so often, was a compromise: part of it had taken place and part of it had not, the Christ had come and yet would come.'[79] Robinson finds the earliest Christology in Acts 3:14–26, which proclaims that God has sent Jesus as servant and prophet, and will send him as Messiah if the Jewish people repent. Thus Jesus is still only the Christ-elect – he is yet to come *as Messiah*. (In order to maintain this view, Robinson has to excise the phrase 'that his Christ should suffer' as a Lucan addition to Peter's speech.) The speech of Acts 2, on the other hand, expresses the later Christology, that Christ has already come (cf. Acts 2:31, 36). These two Christologies were never

---

[75] *Ibid.*, pp. 45f.

[76] For Robinson's full argument for this interpretation, see *ibid.*, pp. 43–51. The interpretation is adopted by, among others, G. S. Duncan, *Jesus, Son of Man* (London, 1947), pp. 175–177; T. F. Glasson, *The Second Advent*, pp. 54–62, V. Taylor, *The Gospel according to St. Mark* (London, 1952), pp. 568f.; R. T. France, *Jesus and the Old Testament* (London, 1971), pp. 140–142.

[77] *Jesus and His Coming*, pp. 26f.   [78] *Ibid.*, p. 28.   [79] *Ibid.*, p. 142 (his italics).

really reconciled by the church, and so there arose the double affirmation, both that Christ has come and that Christ will come.[80]

Elsewhere Robinson speaks of the second advent as a mythological
concept. 'Yet the myth is not free speculation. It is a picture designed
to bring out the true depths, the full implication, of the present
relationship.' The picture of the last things is not historical prediction, but a representation 'to interpret present realities in all their
. . . eschatological quality.'[81] 'Eschatological' has apparently been
denuded of any temporal sense, and means here 'ultimate', 'of final
consequence'. Eschatology has been Platonized.

Although Robinson falls within the tradition of C. H. Dodd, he
prefers to describe his interpretation as 'inaugurated eschatology'
rather than 'realized eschatology'. At the hour of Jesus' death, he
writes, '*all* is inaugurated, yet *only* inaugurated. . . . Thenceforward
men are in the presence of the eschatological event and the eschatological community. . . . What, later, the Church proclaimed was,
not that *all* was *inaugurated*, but that while some elements in it were
now fulfilled, others still lay purely in the future. . . .'[82] Hence the
emergence of the parousia doctrine.

Robinson's critics have drawn attention to four main points. First,
Thiselton asks: 'If the earliest community were accustomed to think
of the parables of crisis as applying to confrontation by the word of
Jesus, why was it not sufficient to re-apply these same parables to
the effects of the evangelistic preaching of the early Church, in which
Jesus, once again, confronted the hearer? Why did they require a
re-application to a *future* parousia, unless of course this was part of
their original purpose?'[83] Like Dodd, Robinson goes too far in elim-
inating the parousia from such parables.

Secondly, Robinson's exegesis of Mark 14:62 is questionable.
Whilst it fits well with the original meaning of Daniel 7:13, it has
not convinced many scholars apart from those British ones listed
above (n. 76). Those who believe that Mark 14:62 does refer to a
future parousia point out, for example, that when *Jews* interpreted
Daniel 7:13 messianically, they did so in terms of a *coming from*

---

[80] *Ibid.*, pp. 140–159. *Cf.* his article 'The Most Primitive Christology of All?' in *Twelve New Testament Studies* (London, 1962), pp. 139–153.
[81] *In the End God* (London, ²1968), pp. 75, 79. *Cf.* the whole chapter, pp. 68–82.
[82] *Jesus and his Coming*, pp. 101f. The whole paragraph should be read.
[83] *TynB* 27, 1976, pp. 42f.

God on the clouds of heaven; that, surely, is how the High Priest who heard Jesus' words would have understood them. Also, it is gratuitous for Robinson to assume that the quotations from Psalm 110:1 and Daniel 7:13 are *parallel* expressions referring to Jesus' vindication after his suffering. Since the reference to his 'sitting' comes *before* the reference to his 'coming', it is more natural to assume that the 'coming' is a distinct event after the 'sitting'.[84]

Thirdly, Robinson's explanation of why Christ came to be expected twice is highly speculative. C. F. D. Moule's criticism of his exegesis of Acts 3:19–21 concludes: 'It is simpler, surely, to interpret the crucial words to mean that Jesus is *already* recognized as the *previously* predestined Christ . . . who at the end is to be sent *back again* into the world.'[85]

Fourthly, it is hard to see how Robinson reconciles his view that Jesus did not expect a parousia with his view that Jesus expected a final consummation. Although claiming that Jesus regarded himself as intimately connected with the final day, he does not clarify Jesus' role in this final consummation. He thus destroys the unity between the different stages of Jesus' redemptive work, from its inception to its consummation.

As for the idea that the parousia is 'mythology', the same questions are appropriate as were asked of Dodd.[86] And Robinson's term 'inaugurated eschatology' is preferable to 'realized eschatology', *as long as* it is taken to include a parousia reference: Jesus, in his ministry, death and resurrection, 'inaugurated' God's saving purpose (which had been anticipated in the Old Testament period) and manifested the kingdom's presence, but that purpose and that kingdom will reach their consummation only at the parousia of the Son of man. The parousia is not something separate from the first coming

---

[84] See A. L. Moore, *The Parousia in the New Testament*, pp. 139f.; G. R. Beasley-Murray, review of *Jesus and his Coming* in *JTS* 10, 1959, pp. 134–140; N. Perrin, *The Kingdom of God in the Teaching of Jesus* (London, 1963), pp. 142–144. Perrin accepts the saying as authentic here, but denies its authenticity in *Rediscovering the Teaching of Jesus* (London, 1967), pp. 173–185. Other scholars who interpret the saying as a reference to the parousia, but deny that Jesus said it, include J. Jeremias, *New Testament Theology*, 1 (ET, London, 1971), pp. 273f.; E. Schweizer, *The Good News according to Mark* (ET, London, 1971), pp. 326f., 331.

[85] 'The Christology of Acts', in L. E. Keck and J. L. Martyn (eds.), *Studies in Luke-Acts* (London, 1968), p. 168 (his italics).

[86] Above, p. 78. For a fuller critique of Robinson's view of the mythological nature of eschatological language, see R. Aldwinkle, *Death in the Secular City* (London, 1972), pp. 120–131.

of Jesus, but the outworking and completion of what was inaugurated then. This is the emphasis of the school of thought to which we now turn.

O. Cullmann, W. G. Kümmel and 'salvation history'

The concept of salvation history (German *Heilsgeschichte*) as a key to the understanding of the biblical message is linked with the names of scholars such as Gerhard von Rad in Germany, Alan Richardson in England and G. Ernest Wright in America. They believe that God's saving purpose is progressively revealed through his actions in history – which the Bible relates and interprets – and, supremely in the 'career' of Jesus Christ. But it is the Swiss theologian Oscar Cullmann especially who has understood eschatology in terms of *Heilsgeschichte*. He expounds his approach in *Christ and Time*.[87]

In opposition to Bultmann's existentialist approach, Cullmann insists that eschatology is 'an absolutely chronological concept'.[88] Jesus and the early Christians took over the Jewish concept of 'linear time', *i.e.* time moving forward from before creation to the parousia and beyond; and envisaged this 'time line' as being punctuated by particular redemptive 'moments' (Greek *kairoi*). But unlike other Jews, Jesus and his followers regarded God's decisive redemptive activity as already taking place in Jesus' own ministry, death and resurrection. That 'appearance of Christ is the decisive event in the time-table of the divine plan'; from that moment 'we are in the final phase', 'the end-time' until the parousia.[89] There is thus a tension between the already fulfilled eschaton and the not yet completed eschatological events. To explain this tension Cullmann uses a metaphor from the Second World War: even though D-Day has occurred and the decisive battle won, the war may continue for some long time until VE-Day. In Jesus' ministry the decisive battle has been won (*cf.* Lk. 10:18; 11:20), but the war will continue until 'Victory Day'.[90] At the end this tension will be resolved in what seems to be for Cullmann a public and cosmic event: he envisages a real parousia

---

[87] Originally published in 1946, its revised English edition (London, 1962) includes an introductory chapter in which Cullmann responds to his critics.
[88] 'The Return of Christ', in *The Early Church* (London, 1956), p. 144.
[89] *Ibid.*, pp. 153, 155.   [90] *Christ and Time*, p. 84

of Christ and a transformed creation. 'This is why Christ will return to earth. The decisive event, like the first decisive event which took place under Pontius Pilate, will take place on earth, because matter itself has to be re-created.'[91]

Cullmann appealed to Kümmel for support for his claim that this temporal tension between present and future is found in authentic teaching of Jesus in the Synoptic Gospels. The thesis of Kümmel's *Promise and Fulfilment* (ET, London, 1957) is that Jesus saw the present as a time of eschatological fulfilment, and believed the time would soon come when what had begun in Jesus would be consummated in him. 'Present and future are related as present fulfilment carrying with it the certainty of future promise.'[92] Kümmel also stands with Cullmann in arguing that Jesus expected an interval, however short, between his death and the parousia.[93] And they agree, against all demythologizing claims to the contrary, that for Jesus 'the future as an actual happening *in time* was something essential', as is proved by the fact that in some texts he 'restricts the imminent coming of the Kingdom of God to the period of the generation of his contemporaries.'[94]

Cullmann's emphasis that the *decisive* eschatological event has already occurred gives him a way of handling those passages where Jesus anticipates the parousia within a generation (Mt. 10:23; Mk. 9:1; 13:30). The presence of salvation during his ministry gave rise to the conviction that the final coming of the kingdom would not be long delayed. (Cullmann's argument is thus exactly opposite to the common view that emphasis on the presence of salvation arose as a substitute for the unfulfilled expectation of an imminent parousia.) This hope of an early parousia proved to be mistaken, but since the basis of expectation is the Christ who has already come, it makes no difference in principle whether the interval between Jesus' death and his parousia is short or long.[95] Kümmel's approach is similar, but he suggests that Jesus was using 'the imagery of his time (*i.e.*, the

---

[91] *The Early Church*, p. 147; cf. p. 156; *Christ and Time*, pp. 141–143.
[92] N. Perrin's summary (*The Kingdom of God in the Teaching of Jesus*, p. 88) of W. G. Kümmel, *Promise and Fulfilment*, pp. 141–155.
[93] W. G. Kümmel, *Promise and Fulfilment*, pp. 64–83; O. Cullmann, *Christ and Time*, p. 149.
[94] W. G. Kümmel, *Promise and Fulfilment*, p. 146; cf. p. 148, and O. Cullmann, *The Early Church*, p. 144; *Christ and Time*, p. xix.
[95] *Christ and Time*, pp. 85–88.

language of imminent expectation) to describe the *nearness* of the Kingdom of God in order to clothe *in living words* the certainty of God's redemptive action directed towards the consummation.' The *imminent* expectation, therefore, need not be repeated nowadays, but the *future* expectation is indispensable, 'because in this form alone can the nature of God's redemptive action *in history* be held fast'.[96]

For both scholars, then, the tension between present and future is fundamental. And the parousia as a genuinely future event is an essential part of God's saving plan. Only at his return to earth will Christ's role as the Mediator of salvation be complete: 'from the creation to the new creation the whole course of the work of God has Christ as its centre.'[97]

Critics of Cullmann were not slow to come forward. Some of their arguments, beginning with those of Bultmann, are given here.[98]

a. In his review of *Christ and Time*, Bultmann accepts that a salvation-history scheme is present in Luke-Acts, but rejects Cullmann's claim that it can be found throughout the New Testament, or in the teaching of Jesus.[99]

b. In the New Testament Christ is not the 'mid-point of history', but rather the 'end of history' (*cf.* Gal. 4:4).[100]

c. Cullmann's 'solution' to the problem of the delayed parousia serves only to trivialize it – the delay has after all lasted 1900 years![101]

d. Bultmann dismisses the contention that the 'time-line' is basic for the New Testament writers: 'to say that the essential point of the words, "the Reign of God is at hand", does indeed have to do with chronology, only not in the sense that the nearness of the end is emphasized, but rather that a new division of time is proclaimed (pp. 87ff.) is a tortured expedient in face of embarrassment.'[102]

---

[96] *Promise and Fulfilment*, pp. 152f. (his italics).

[97] *The Early Church*, p. 145; *cf.* pp. 145–149, and *Christ and Time*, p. 109. In referring to Christ's role in creation Cullmann is, of course, going beyond the recorded teaching of Jesus and interpreting the more developed Christology of some New Testament writers.

[98] My discussion of course concentrates on the eschatological aspect of Cullmann's scheme, though it is in fact difficult to separate from the rest.

[99] 'History of Salvation and History', ET in *Existence and Faith* (London, 1961), pp. 234f. The thesis that it was Luke who first introduced the salvation history scheme into what was previously a Gospel of futurist imminent eschatology is expounded in H. Conzelmann, *The Theology of St. Luke* (ET, London, 1960).

[100] *Existence and Faith*, p. 237.   [101] *Ibid.*, pp. 237f.   [102] *Ibid.*, p. 238.

e. James Barr has objected to Cullmann's thesis on linguistic grounds. In *The Semantics of Biblical Language* (London, 1961) he attacked Kittel's *Theological Dictionary of the New Testament* for its tendency to deduce the meanings of words from their etymology rather than from their context. Then in *Biblical Words for Time* (London, ²1969) he criticized Cullmann in particular for the way in which he emphasized the distinction between the two Greek words *kairos* and *aiōn* in building up his interpretation of the biblical concept of time.

f. J. Macquarrie admires Cullmann's work as 'an elucidation of the biblical understanding of such concepts as "time", "history", and so on', but is alarmed at his assumption that we must accept this biblical view ourselves. For we cannot accept the biblical scheme as Cullmann presents it except by surrendering 'the hard-won distinctions which thought has made among such concepts as "time", "process", "history", "myth" '.[103]

Cullmann responded briefly to some of these points in the introductory chapter to the 1962 edition of *Christ and Time*. Then he published a larger work, *Salvation in History* (ET, London, 1967) in which he expounded his viewpoint, sometimes with different arguments from those used in the earlier volume. His reaction to the criticisms listed above is as follows.

a. A large part of *Salvation in History* is taken up with an attempt to show that the salvation history theme and the 'already–not yet' tension are characteristic not merely of certain parts of the New Testament but of all major New Testament writers and of Jesus himself. In authentic sayings of Jesus we find evidence that he thought of the kingdom of God as both already present (*e.g.*, Mt. 11:2ff.; Mk. 3:27; Lk. 10:18; 11:20) and not yet consummated (*e.g.*, Mt. 6:10; Mk. 1:15; 8:38; 9:1; 14:25).[104] The tension between these two sets of sayings – each of which presupposes the other – is the really new thing in Jesus' eschatology. And it is 'the beginning of a salvation history. It is *characteristic of all New Testament salvation history that between Christ's resurrection and his return there is an interval the essence of which is determined by this tension.*'[105] There may be a difference of *perspective* between Jesus' message and the

---

[103] *The Scope of Demythologizing*, p. 62.   [104] *Salvation in History*, pp. 194–201.
[105] *Ibid.*, p. 202 (his italics).

developed scheme of Luke-Acts, but in *principle* both operate in terms of salvation history.[106] Cullmann then offers evidence to suggest that, despite the differences of emphasis, a salvation history perspective is important for primitive Christianity, Paul, and even John.[107]

b. Cullmann protests that the claim that in the New Testament Christ is not the mid-point but the end of history is based on a misunderstanding. He meant simply that the Christ-event was the *decisive* moment in God's developing plan of salvation, and that is surely firmly enough based in the New Testament.[108]

c. Bultmann, like many other scholars, has exaggerated the problem caused by the delay of the parousia. There are, after all, only three texts in the Synoptics where the interval before the parousia is limited to Jesus' generation (Mt. 10:23; Mk. 9:1; 13:30); and there is no evidence elsewhere that the delay created a *problem*, except 2 Peter 3:3f. and John 21:23. There is no hint in the epistles of the disappointment which the non-arrival of the parousia is supposed by Bultmann and others to have created.[109] Despite this rejoinder, there are many who question whether Cullmann can afford to be quite so indifferent to the seemingly endless extension of the interim period.

d. Cullmann accuses Bultmann of failing to distinguish between the question of the time of the end (limiting the interval to Jesus' generation) and that of temporality in general. The fact that the early church's expectation of an imminent parousia proved to be mistaken does not mean that the whole notion of the futurity of the end collapses. To remove the time element from eschatology is to exchange a distinctively biblical perspective for the subjectivity of existential decision. Bultmann is arbitrarily inconsistent when he retains the 'scandal' of the cross as an objective, divine saving event, but demythologizes the temporality of eschatology.[110]

One may comment here that Bultmann and Cullmann are perhaps not so far apart as their debate might suggest. Cullmann's willingness to use a 'flexible' notion of time in his treatment of the 'imminence'

[106] *Ibid.*, p. 181. *Cf.* I. H. Marshall, *Luke – Historian and Theologian* (Exeter, 1970), pp. 130–136; E. E. Ellis, *Eschatology in Luke* (Philadelphia, 1972).

[107] *Salvation in History*, pp. 236–291. For a concise survey of evidence that the salvation history perspective is not Luke's invention but is found throughout the New Testament, see A. L. Moore, *The Parousia in the New Testament*, pp. 82–91.   [108] *Christ and Time*, pp. xxf.

[109] *Salvation in History*, pp. 241f.; *cf.* pp. 218–220.   [110] *Ibid.*, p. 180; *cf.* pp. 319ff.

texts indicates that he is moving towards a kind of demythologizing. When he says that 'the preaching of the nearness of the kingdom determines the present more than it characterizes the future',[111] he is not very far from Bultmann's interpretation of eschatology in terms of 'our permanent availability for existential decision'.[112] But whereas Cullmann asserts that decision is only meaningful as response to God's gracious activity, which is something external to ourselves, Bultmann seems more ready to blur this distinction between the subjective self and the objective action of God.

e. Barr overstated Cullmann's reliance on word-study (as opposed to context) in establishing a distinction between *kairos* and *aiōn*. In any case, Cullmann was not setting out to offer a philosophy of history or a 'doctrine' of time (as many critics supposed), but simply to clarify the Bible's 'popular' idea of time as a background to the already–not yet tension.[113]

f. Cullmann counters the argument that the salvation history is incompatible with a modern world view by observing that it was equally unacceptable in ancient times. The notion of salvation history was just as offensive to Paul's Athenians as it is today, and yet Paul, together with other early Christians, insisted on it. Indeed, the decisive debate in the ancient church 'consisted in its successful *resistance against the Gnostic attempt* to eliminate the salvation history of the Bible by philosophical reinterpretation'.[114] Clearly there are questions here which need to be debated further. Is Cullmann right to claim that the salvation-history scheme is an essential part of the gospel, like the cross and resurrection? Is he so concerned to stress salvation history as a basic theme in the New Testament that he underplays the great variety of ways in which New Testament writers express the gospel? How far should 'the modern world-view' be allowed to determine what theological formulations are 'acceptable'? *Precisely* what insights of modern study does Macquarrie feel are threatened by adherence to salvation history?

We may fairly conclude that, of all the approaches to the coming of the kingdom and the parousia discussed here, Cullmann's comes closest to the teaching of the New Testament and of Jesus himself.

---

[111] *The Early Church*, p. 153.
[112] *Cf.* J. M. Robinson's review of *The Early Church* in *JBL* 76, 1957, p. 173.
[113] *Christ and Time*, pp. xxiv-xxxi.   [114] *Salvation in History*, pp. 22f.; *cf.* pp. 319ff.

But that gives no grounds for complacency over the problems of communicating that teaching and handling it in relation to modern knowledge and modern world-views. As J. P. Martin remarks in his perceptive review of *Salvation in History*, Cullmann needs a philosopher, for it is in the realm of philosophy that Bultmann, for all his defects, scores heavily against him.[115]

Conclusions

The foregoing discussion hardly captures that blend of joyful anticipation and solemn urgency which the message of the parousia breathes into the New Testament. The scholarly debate is too intricate, the differences of opinion too numerous, for that. And yet there are important lessons which we cannot ignore.

'Realized eschatology' and 'inaugurated eschatology' are right in their emphasis that with the coming of Jesus the salvation of God came to men in a new way: the kingdom of God had arrived. Yet their abolition of the parousia leaves unanswered the question of the future of Jesus Christ, and the question of the goal of history.

Bultmann's demythologizing is right to stress that eschatology is pointless unless it affects the life of the individual. Yet it is fatally individualistic and cannot help us with a theology of history or of the natural world. This is why the cosmic perspective, which was characteristic of apocalyptic thought, is essential. God's purposes are not only concerned with the individual. The future is not merely the future of the individual, but the future of Christ, and of God's purposes for the universe. And the New Testament's stress on the *public* nature of the parousia has its place. Is it wrong for the church – conscious that Christ is so often hidden from men, so often misunderstood – to long for a moment of *public* visitation and *public* vindication?

Cullmann's approach seems to me to do most justice to the New Testament data, and to be defensible against most of the criticisms which we have just considered. I would not myself, however, speak exactly as he does about Jesus' being mistaken over the timing of the parousia. Whilst I agree with him that Mark 9:1; 13:30 and

---

[115] *Interpretation* 20, 1966, p. 345. (It is a review of the German original, published in 1965.)

Matthew 10:23 presuppose that the coming of the kingdom is imminent, I think that a better solution to the problem which these texts pose is possible if one recognizes that the same problem of imminence is found right through biblical prophecy and apocalyptic. In the Bible, prophets repeatedly foretell God's acts of salvation and judgment in a way which suggests that the great day of fulfilment is imminent. In a literal and total sense, such prophecies remain unfulfilled. But they are affirming that each crisis, each blessing which follows the words of the prophet is a partial realization within history of the ultimate victory of God. Even if this ultimate victory, which we call the parousia, is delayed, the shadow of Christ's eschatological presence began already to fall in the period inaugurated by his ministry, death and resurrection. The imminence language of Jesus asserts that the age of the decisive fulfilment has really dawned, the kingdom of God is being manifested here and now, and the present manifestations guarantee God's ultimate triumph through Christ.[116]

Although Cullmann offers (in nearly all respects) a faithful account of New Testament eschatology, his failure to discuss this in relation to modern questions about the nature of reality and about biblical hermeneutics is frustrating. How does he think the New Testament writers *envisaged* the parousia? How does *he* envisage it? These are questions which he seems content not to ask. But do they not have to be asked?

Admittedly, they are very difficult to answer. For much of the New Testament language is allusive – symbolic or pictorial if not 'mythological'. This is to be expected, since it refers (like the creation stories) to an event which is unparalleled and which has not been witnessed by human beings. In any case, Jesus and the New Testament writers are always less concerned to speak of *how* the parousia will take place than they are to assert the *reasons* for it and its *meaning* for faith. But it seems to me important to assert the following. God, who has acted in history in Jesus and has thereby demonstrated his loving, saving purpose, will at the end of history bring his saving purpose to completion by the parousia of Christ. Christ will reveal himself as Judge and Saviour to all men, past, present and

---

[116] See my article in *TynB* 30, 1979, and works cited in notes 50 and 51 there; see also above, p. 22.

future. He will welcome all who are 'in Christ' into his presence, in an eternal kingdom which will transcend space and time as we at present experience them. The parousia will thus be an event marking the climax of our present historical order, but will itself be beyond history in that it will introduce a new order discontinuous with the present course of history. It is a genuinely future event, a real meeting between a real Christ and a real community of persons. It will be the public and triumphant manifestation of the hitherto hidden presence of God's rule in Jesus, the ultimate vindication of God's purposes in him.[117]

The 'tension' in eschatology for which Cullmann and Kümmel argue is very important for Christian thought. It enables us to acknowledge the ambiguities, the failures, the conflicts of present experience, without surrendering hope and 'faith in the God of promise'.[118] It is significant that when Paul was confronted with the excessively 'realized' eschatology of the Corinthian enthusiasts, he responded by insisting, in apocalyptic language, that Christ is yet to come, and only then will the *complete* blessings of God be given (*cf.* 1 Cor. 4:5, with 4:8–13; 15:20–34). This balance between 'already' and 'not yet' is essential for Christian thinking and Christian living, and the discovery of it in the New Testament has been one of the real gains of biblical scholarship in the last few decades.[119]

Finally, one issue comes to mind where real gains very much need to be made in the coming decades. This is in the understanding of mythological and pictorial language in eschatology. If there is ever to be greater rapport and more agreement between the kind of 'literalist' writer mentioned at the beginning of the chapter, and the scholar who is firmly committed to widescale demythologizing, there will have to be a more careful and sympathetic assessment of the

---

[117] *Cf.* R. Aldwinckle, *Death in the Secular City*, pp. 128f.

[118] A frequent theme in J. Moltmann's *Theology of Hope* (ET, London, 1967).

[119] Admittedly, there are still scholars, mostly of the Bultmann school, who argue that according to Jesus the kingdom was not present, but imminent: see *e.g.*, H. Conzelmann, 'Present and Future in the Synoptic Tradition', *JTC* 5, 1968, pp. 26–44. But the weight of evidence is surely with those who argue that in Jesus' teaching the kingdom is both present and future, *e.g.* Cullmann, Kümmel, Ladd, Schnackenburg and their works already cited in this chapter. This view is also held now by R. H. Fuller: in *The Foundations of New Testament Christology* (London, 1965), pp. 103f., he admits that the 'proleptic eschatology' (a perspective similar to Conzelmann's) which he advocated in *The Mission and Achievement of Jesus* (London, 1954) arose from his over-reaction against Dodd's position.

nature and extent of myth, image, metaphor in the New Testament The 'demythologizer' needs to be convinced that the 'literalist' can take the nature of pre-scientific language and thought-forms seriously. And the 'literalist' needs to be convinced that the 'demythologizer' is not determined to impose on the New Testament message a philosophical framework which he has already adopted for other reasons. Too often on both sides the interpretation has been done without prior declaration or testing of the principles of interpretation.[120]

---

[120] There is some discussion of principles by Karl Rahner in *Sacramentum Mundi*, 2, pp. 242–246; and in 'The Hermeneutics of Eschatological Assertions', in *Theological Investigations*, 4 (ET, London, 1966), pp. 323–346; and R. Aldwinckle, *Death in the Secular City*, pp. 120–131. It will be clear that in my view more justice is done to the biblical message by scholars such as Cullmann, Aldwinckle and those listed on p. 22, above, than by both the over-literalists and those who demythologize the future.

Chapter Six

The future life: resurrection and immortality

In days when the words of Scripture were accepted by most Christians as straightforward divine revelations, belief in life after death was no problem. The reality of eternal life was guaranteed by 1 Corinthians 15 and by Jesus' promise of 'many mansions'. Nowadays the situation is not so simple. Yet it still comes as a surprise to discover a number of Christian theologians who are indifferent or even hostile to the possibility of human existence beyond death. I shall refer to some of them briefly before surveying the contributions of some theologians who have attempted to expound and to defend the reasonableness of Christian belief in life after death. Finally in this chapter I shall draw some conclusions from their discussions, and suggest ways in which the New Testament's message about eternal life may be understood today.

The future life as a problem for Christian thought

Rudolf Bultmann, concerned as he was with the Christian's *present*, believed the hope for a future life is 'not merely unintelligible for modern man, it is completely meaningless.'[1] The American G. D. Kaufman believes that since the consciousness of individuals is bound up with their bodily existence, 'we have no reason to suppose that their life continues beyond the grave.' Jesus' resurrection appearances were in fact hallucinations convincing the disciples that God's purposes in history would be continued despite the crucifixion; no doctrine of human resurrection can be built upon the supposed resurrection of Jesus. 'To have faith in God is precisely to give one's

---

[1] H. Zahrnt's summary of Bultmann's viewpoint in *The Question of God* (ET, London, 1969), p. 218.

eternal destiny over into his hands, to do with however he sees fit.' 'Though he slay me, yet will I trust him' (Jb. 13:15 AV) is the appropriate radical Christian stance. Underlying this viewpoint is Kaufman's scepticism about the New Testament's understanding of Jesus' resurrection, and his emphasis on certain Old Testament insights, and early ones at that – true though they be – at the expense of the later additional insights of the New Testament. Thus, he stresses the Hebrew view of man as a psychosomatic unity (and its similarity to modern unitary views of man), and claims that the primary concern of the Bible and of theology is God's ongoing purpose *within history*.[2]

Jürgen Moltmann, despite his being a 'theologian of hope', seems to deny life after death. Many times in *Theology of Hope* he uses biblical and traditional imagery of 'parousia' and 'new creation' in an apparently literal way.[3] Yet it becomes clearer from *The Crucified God* that he questions the notion of a future life because it produces a 'resigned attitude to life'.[4] 'Resurrection life is not a further life after death': rather, resurrection symbolizes the total consummation of history, 'after' which there is only God.[5] His 'theology of hope', a theology of politics and of God's ongoing work in history, has thus led him to rule out a life after death for the individual. His motives are understandable, but what account can he give of the experience of those who live and die outside the scope of the political and social change which he rightly stresses? What is 'hope' for them?[6] However, Moltmann's thought is so complex, not to say obscure, that it would be rash to charge him with flat denial of life after death.

Some other theologians make explicit claims to believe in a future life, yet express their belief in very un-traditional terms. Paul Tillich speaks of immortality not in terms of individual destinies, but as immortality within the 'eternal memory'; but his thought, too, is

[2] *Systematic Theology: A Historicist Perspective* (New York, 1968), pp. 455–474 (quotations from pp. 464, 469).
[3] See J. Hick, *Death and Eternal Life* (London, 1976), pp. 213–215.
[4] *Theology of Hope*, p. 208.
[5] *The Crucified God* (ET, London, 1974), pp. 169f., 278.
[6] See the discussion of Moltmann by S. W. Sykes, who also mentions other more philosophical motives for Moltmann's viewpoint, in 'Life after Death: the Christian Doctrine of Heaven', in R. W. A. McKinney (ed.), *Creation, Christ and Culture: Studies in Honour of T. F. Torrance* (Edinburgh, 1976), pp. 255–260.

obscure and sometimes self-contradictory.[7] The process theologian Charles Hartshorne also believes that when we are dead our lives will be perpetually remembered by God, as does David Edwards.[8] Like Kaufman, Edwards rejects any suggestion that man has a 'soul' which could survive the body's death. He therefore speaks of eternal life as 'God's memory of us' rather than as the resurrection of individuals – though in a footnote he claims to have a concept of 'personal' or 'subjective' survival.[9]

According to these and other writers, the main obstacle to belief in a traditional doctrine of life after death is the modern understanding of man as unitary, so that it seems unreasonable to believe either in an immortal soul which survives the death of the body or in the resurrection of a body which obviously disintegrates after death.[10] But can a system of belief which is ambiguous about life after death be legitimately labelled 'Christian'? Or is Austin Farrer right to protest that 'Christianity cannot for any length of time survive the amputation of such a limb as life to come?'[11] Let us, then, consider how some other writers have articulated belief in a future life. This chapter will first survey the modern discussion (much of which involves philosophical issues as well as exegetical and theological ones). It will then look briefly at the question of the 'intermediate state'. Finally, it will suggest a way of expressing belief in life after death which takes account of the biblical teaching and of the wider issues raised in this chapter.

Resurrection or immortality?

A significant area of debate has been whether Christian hope is more

---

[7] Systematic Theology, 3 (London, 1964), pp. 399f. See J. Hick, Death and Eternal Life, pp. 215–217.

[8] On Hartshorne, see J. Hick, ibid., pp. 217–221. For Edward's view see his The Last Things Now (London, 1969), esp. pp. 88–91. Pannenberg seems to take a similar line though his thought is extremely difficult to follow: see J. Hick, Death and Eternal Life, pp. 221–226; A. D. Galloway, Wolfhart Pannenberg, pp. 93–98.

[9] The Last Things Now, p. 92, n. 9.

[10] Others observe that since individuality involves space and time, individual existence seems impossible beyond our space-time continuum. See the discussion of various writers including those mentioned above, in R. Aldwinckle, Death in the Secular City (London, 1972), pp. 88–96; P. Badham, 'Recent Thinking on Christian Beliefs, VI. The Future Life', ExpT 88, 1976–77, pp. 197–199.

[11] A Celebration of Faith (London, 1970), p. 165.

properly expressed in terms of resurrection or of immortality. Oscar Cullmann provoked urgent discussion with his pamphlet *Immortality of the Soul or Resurrection of the Dead?*[12] Here he contrasted Jesus' shrinking from death – because for Jesus death was an enemy – with Socrates' quiet acceptance of it. And he stressed the contrast between 'Greek' anthropology, according to which man's soul is naturally immortal and lives on after the body's death, and Judeo-Christian anthropology which regards man as a psychosomatic unity, so that life after death must be understood as resurrection of the whole man. In the New Testament there is no talk of anyone but God being 'naturally immortal'; if man is to survive death it must be because God in his grace gives him a resurrection body analogous to Christ's resurrection body. This resurrection body will be given not at death but at the parousia. Thanks not least to Cullmann, it has now become a commonplace among scholars and popular writers that resurrection rather than immortality is the proper Christian description of the nature of the after-life. And it has obvious advantages: it is more akin to biblical language, it stresses that life after death is a gift of God rather than a natural 'possession' of man, it asserts that our personality and individuality will be maintained in the after-life.[13]

The argument, however, is not over. The assumptions of Cullmann and his supporters have been questioned on three grounds, partly exegetical and partly philosophical.

a. Greek and Hebrew thought cannot be so sharply distinguished. In a critique of Cullmann, G. W. E. Nickelsburg, Jr, observes that a 'Greek' view of immortality seems to underlie Jewish books such as Wisdom of Solomon, Testament of Asher, 4 Maccabees, 1 Enoch 103–104, Jubilees 23 and the Dead Sea Scrolls.[14]

---

[12] ET, London, 1958. In the preface to the ET he comments, 'No other publication of mine has provoked such enthusiasm or such violent hostility' (p. 5).

[13] H. Thielicke adds that the reality of death is denied if part of us is immortal: 'Resurrection: that is the grave burst open. . . . Immortality: that is the grave denied' (*Tod und Leben* [Tübingen, ²1946], p. 100; cf. p. 182). Cf. M. Wiles, *The Remaking of Christian Doctrine* (London, 1974), pp. 125–146, who discusses various arguments in favour of 'resurrection' language, though he does not think them conclusive.

[14] *Resurrection, Immortality and Eternal Life in Intertestamental Judaism* (London, 1972), pp. 177–180. See also H. C. C. Cavallin, *Life After Death: Paul's Argument for the Resurrection of the Dead in 1 Corinthians 15, Part 1: An Enquiry into the Jewish Background* (Lund, 1974); and J. Barr, *Old and New in Interpretation* (London, 1964), pp. 52–64.

b. A resurrected body requires an environment or a 'space' in which to function. Yet we have no reason to believe that there are resurrected bodies functioning in 'our space'. Nor have we any means of knowing whether there is 'another space' in which resurrected bodies might function.

c. Since (it is argued) we must reject the old notion that God literally resurrects dead persons by collecting and re-animating the particles of which their physical bodies were made, any talk of 'resurrection' necessarily involves us in speaking of a 'soul' or 'person' which survives physical death and receives the new resurrection body. Hence the doctrines of 'resurrection' and 'immortality' are not as opposed to each other as is commonly believed.[15]

This last point has been stressed by Maurice Wiles in an appendix to *The Remaking of Christian Doctrine*. Whilst admitting that resurrection is a richer symbol than immortality, he claims that 'immortality' language can in practice safeguard all that 'resurrection' language is said to safeguard. It is perfectly possible to speak, as many patristic writers did, of immortality as a gift of God rather than as a natural characteristic or achievement of man. It is idle to claim that a body is necessary for self-expression, since we believe God is bodiless, yet we ascribe to him both existence and self-expression. And since the postulated resurrection body cannot be our physical body reconstituted, the notion of resurrection cannot be the useful symbol of continuity between this life and the next which it is sometimes claimed to be.[16]

Among writers who refuse to come down firmly in favour of either 'resurrection' or 'immortality' are Russell Aldwinckle and Murray Harris. Aldwinckle observes that both terms need a good deal of defining and safeguarding against misunderstanding, while Harris shows how 'immortality', as well as 'resurrection', is a thoroughly biblical term – though he insists on certain basic differences between biblical and Platonic thought on immortality.[17]

---

[15] On these last two points see P. Badham, *ExpT* 88, p. 199.

[16] See further M. Wiles, *The Remaking of Christian Doctrine*, pp. 125–146. S. R. Sutherland also argues that the supposed advantages of 'resurrection' over 'immortality' are more apparent than real, in 'Immortality and Resurrection', *Religious Studies* 3, 1967–68, pp. 377–389.

[17] R. Aldwinckle, *Death in the Secular City*, pp. 82–100, esp. p. 88. M. Harris, 'Resurrection and Immortality: Eight Theses', *Themelios* 1.2, Spring 1976, pp. 50–55. This is an excellent brief survey and synthesis of New Testament teaching.

But how can an after-life be conceived? The philosopher H. H. Price has offered two pictures of an after-life, one embodied and the other disembodied.[18] An *embodied* after-life would require a 'material' world with spatial attributes, though the space need not be three-dimensional or the geometry Euclidean. This 'world' might be in 'another space' than our own, or in this space, but in another dimension of which our present senses are unaware. The main problem in postulating a *disembodied* after-life is the problem of conceiving what experiences an immaterial soul could have. But, says Price, since the soul would still have memory, character and the power of imagination, the next world could be a world of vivid mental images, like dreams, which are the product of our memories and desires. A world of images would be perfectly real to the disembodied soul, just as our dreams are, as long as the dream continues, even though the objects in our dreams do not exist in physical space. Nor need a world so envisaged be a totally private world: through telepathy, 'there might be a common image-world which is the joint product of many telepathically interacting personalities.' But probably there would be many next worlds, since telepathic communication would only take place between like-minded personalities: each group of like-minded personalities would have a different next world.

Price believes that both these pictures are intelligible and coherent, and suggests that the truth might lie between the two. In the first theory we start from a physical analogy and adjust it, for example, with regard to spatial properties. In the second, we start from a psychological analogy and adjust it, for example, by bringing in telepathy to ensure that the next world is not entirely private and subjective.

Reflecting on Price's second picture, of a 'disembodied' after-life, we may wonder how far personalities will have to be like-minded in order to be able to communicate with each other. If two persons have very similar positive desires, but quite different negative or sinful desires, will they be able to communicate or not? So will they

[18] 'Two Conceptions of the Next World' in *Essays in the Philosophy of Religion* (London, 1972), pp. 98–117; *cf.* his article 'Survival and the Idea of "Another World" ', reprinted in J. R. Smythies (ed.), *Brain and Mind* (London, 1965), pp. 1–24. There are valuable critiques of Price in H. D. Lewis, *The Self and Immortality* (London, 1973), pp. 142–156; and J. Hick, *Death and Eternal Life*, pp. 265–277.

share the same 'world' or not? Nor is there anything particularly religious about Price's theory: it is in fact partly informed by his interest in psychic phenomena. But its importance lies in its attempt to show that there are intelligible and coherent ways of conceiving of an after-life, and in this Price is widely judged to have been successful.

John Hick: a 'global' theology of eternal life

John Hick's *Death and Eternal Life* (London, 1976) is one of the most significant English theological works of the decade. Hick had already written much in support of his conviction that 'any religious understanding of human existence – not merely of one's own existence but of the life of humanity as a whole – positively requires some kind of immortality belief and would be radically incoherent without it.'[19] In *Faith and Knowledge* he presented his 'eschatological verification principle' – summarized in a much-quoted 'parable'. This aims to establish that the statement 'God exists', is factually true-or-false, by showing that the Christian concept of God involves eschatological expectations which will be either fulfilled or not fulfilled.[20] In *Evil and the God of Love* he argued that eternal life is essential for theodicy. Evil and suffering in this world can be reconciled with belief in a loving God only if we presume that this world is 'a vale of soul-making': God's purpose is to use present sufferings and struggles to prepare men for his ultimate kingdom, which will be 'an infinite good that would render worthwhile *any* finite sufferings endured in the course of attaining to it.'[21] Now in *Death and Eternal Life* he draws together some earlier thoughts and offers a comprehensive study, taking insights from parapsychology and Eastern religions as well as from the Christian tradition. The book is offered, he says, as 'a Christian contribution to global or human theology'.[22] Hick's discussion is very wide-ranging, but we can only consider some of the significant points here.

Hick denies that belief in life after death results from wishful

[19] *Ibid.*, p. 11.
[20] *Faith and Knowledge* (London, ²1966), pp. 176–199; the parable is on pp. 177f.
[21] *Evil and the God of Love* (London, 1966), p. 377.
[22] *Death and Eternal Life*, p. 27.

thinking: in many cultures the future life is dreaded rather than longed for.[23]

He thinks the findings of parapsychology are important for investigation into life after death, and they support the view (which he believes plausible on philosophical grounds) that the mind or 'soul' is distinguishable from the brain and may survive the death of the brain. But, he says, psychical research yields little information of religious value about the after-life.[24]

What, then, is the significance of New Testament teaching and the resurrection of Jesus? Clearly, writes Hick, 'something happened' which came to be called the resurrection of Jesus. But we cannot be sure what happened.[25] Some interpreters believe that Jesus' mysteriously transformed body actually rose from the tomb; others believe that the disciples saw visions of the exalted Lord, and interpreted them in terms of resurrection from the dead (a model already familiar to them from Jewish apocalyptic). But the significance of the resurrection does not depend on the outcome of debate over these two views. What was important was God's exaltation of Jesus, and his being alive: and both these facts were established by the earliest Christians on the basis of Jesus' resurrection appearances.

Since Jesus and the early Christians already believed in life after death before, and independently of, Jesus' resurrection, his resurrection can hardly be a primary ground for belief in a life to come. But his resurrection 'does of course support and confirm belief in the continuity of man's life beyond physical death.'[26] And since belief in life after death was already presupposed by Jesus and the early Christians, there is little explicit teaching in the New Testament about its nature. But there is Jesus' reply to the Sadducees (Mk. 12:25), which implies a kind of 'spiritual body'; and there is 1 Corinthians 15. Hick here cites M. E. Dahl,[27] who divided interpre-

---

[23] *Ibid.*, pp. 55–62. *Cf.* John Baillie's classic study, *And the Life Everlasting* (London, 1934), and his statement: 'Nobody ever wanted an endless quantity of life, until discovery had been made of a new and quite particular and exceptional quality of life' (*ibid.*, p. 205).

[24] *Ibid.*, pp. 112–146. On the controversy over 'mind/brain identity', see below, pp. 106f. In the two volumes edited by A. Toynbee – *Man's Concern with Death* (London, 1968), *Life after Death* (London, 1976)–there are several essays by authors who believe that psychical research points to the reality of an after-life.

[25] *Death and Eternal Life*, pp. 171ff.

[26] *Ibid.*, p. 179.

[27] M. E. Dahl, *The Resurrection of the Body* (London, 1962).

tations of Paul's teaching on the resurrection body into three categories.

   a. The 'traditional view' is that at the final resurrection the physical bodies of the dead will be raised, but transformed into a mode suitable to their new environment – just as Jesus' physical body was raised as a transformed glorious body. This view presupposes that Jesus' tomb was empty on 'the third day', and that the general resurrection will be analogous to Jesus' resurrection. It stresses the *continuity* implied in Paul's metaphor (1 Cor. 15:36ff.): the sown seed is indeed transformed into wheat.

   b. The 'accepted' view (*i.e.*, accepted by most scholars today) maintains that the resurrection body is a different body given by God, but expressing the personality within its new environment as the physical body has expressed it on earth. This view accepts that when we die our physical bodies disintegrate and cannot be reconstituted. It does not necessitate belief in the empty tomb. It stresses that when Paul uses the word 'body' (*sōma*) he normally means 'the whole personality' rather than the physical body in distinction from the mind, so that it is not the physical body, but the 'personality' which is raised and re-embodied. There is thus discontinuity of body, but continuity of personality – a view which Paul's seed-harvest metaphor is believed to express well.[28]

   c. Dahl himself, making use of 'the Semitic totality concept', suggests that 'although the resurrection body will not be *materially identical* with the one we now possess, it will be what I choose to call *somatically identical.*'[29] This looks like a compromise between views *a.* and *b.* but as Hick says, it is not at all clear what Dahl means by 'somatic identity', nor precisely how it differs from the other two views.[30]

   Hick himself believes that view *b.* is a coherent possibility, consonant with the modern concept of man as a psycho-physical unity. It can be understood today, Hick suggests, in terms of his 'replica'

[28] The idea that *sōma* in Paul means 'the whole person' or 'personality' has been popularized particularly by R. Bultmann, *New Testament Theology*, 1 (ET, London, 1951), pp. 192–203, and J. A. T. Robinson, *The Body* (London, 1952). It has recently been strongly attacked by R. H. Gundry, *Sōma in Biblical Theology* (Cambridge, 1976).

[29] *The Resurrection of the Body*, p. 10 (his italics).

[30] See *Death and Eternal Life*, p. 186 and n. 47. Dahl *may* be right, that Paul's view lay in between views *a.* and *b.* but his term 'somatic identity' is of doubtful use in clarifying the issue.

theory, according to which resurrection involves 'the divine creation in another space of an exact psycho-physical "replica" of the deceased person.' ('Replica' appears in inverted commas to indicate that there is only one replica, and that it exists only subsequently, not simultaneously with the original.)[31] It is logically possible, he argues, for there to be any number of worlds, each in its own space, all these worlds being observed by God, but only one of them observed by an embodied being who is part of it. The idea of bodily resurrection requires two (or more) such worlds, a person at death (or later) being re-created in another world or space. The pattern of a body can be regarded as a message that is capable of being encoded, transmitted and decoded, and being recognizably the same body.[32] The replica would be identical to the dead person in physical appearance and in character, and would have memory of his former life. Therefore he would naturally think of himself as being the same person as the one who died. So personal continuity and identity is ensured, even though there is no literal physical continuity between the earthly person and the 'replica'.[33]

How, then, does this understanding of resurrection fit into Hick's overall view of life after death? He rejects the idea that men enter into their eternal destiny instantaneously at death, on the grounds that such a scheme is too simple, and does not allow for the fact that human personality must develop freely and gradually if genuine 'person-making' is to take place.[34] This opens the way for a scheme which Hick calls 'pareschatology' – the doctrine of how man progresses from death to the ultimate state (the latter being the concern of eschatology). For, whilst rejecting doctrines of reincarnation as normally conceived, he is attracted to the idea of a series of 're-incarnations' in other worlds.[35]

Hick suggests, then, that at death we temporarily enter into a

[31] *Ibid.*, p. 279.
[32] See *Ibid.*, pp. 280–285, for Hick's discussion and illustrations demonstrating the logical possibility of this. H. D. Lewis has a helpful discussion of Hick's theory in *The Self and Immortality*, pp. 156–162.
[33] Terence Penelhum argues that since Hick's theory does not involve literal physical continuity we cannot be sure of personal identity between the person who died and the 'replica' (*Survival and Disembodied Existence* [London, 1970], pp. 100f.). But Penelhum overplays the need for physical continuity. See *Death and Eternal Life*, pp. 289–295 for Hick's reply to some other criticisms.
[34] *Ibid.*, pp. 238–240, 407–414.   [35] *Ibid.*, pp. 297–396.

mind-dependent world as described by H. H. Price, in the *Tibetan Book of the Dead* and in reports by western spiritualists. We then proceed to a series of embodied existences in other worlds, in our growth towards perfection. Ultimately we shall arrive at what Christian mysticism calls 'the unitive state', what in Hinduism is called 'absorption into the infinite consciousness' and in Buddhism 'nirvana'. In their respective religious traditions these terms do not necessarily imply the extinction of individual personality. Rather, our ultimate state will involve 'a plurality of centres of consciousness, and yet these will not be private but will each include the others in a full mutual sharing constituting the atman, the complex collective consciousness of humanity.'[36] This state of being is probably not embodied, and probably outside time. It is what Christian mysticism has called the Vision of God.

Hick's book is magnificent in its comprehensiveness, remarkable in its careful consideration of all kinds of religious traditions. But Paul Badham, a former pupil of Hick, has criticized his 'replica' theory of resurrection.[37] His argument runs as follows. Although the hypothesis of a plurality of 'spaces' is logically possible, Hick's 'exact replica' must by definition exhibit the same characteristics as the present body, and must therefore be in 'our space' rather than in 'another space'. Hick's theory might therefore be maintained if we speak of the replica's being created in another place (but in our spatial system) – presumably in another galaxy too far to reach by rocket. But the notion of an *'exact* replica' must also be jettisoned, since it leads to ludicrous questions about whether the replica will include the dead person's heart pace-maker, artificial knee-joint, false teeth and glasses. It is better to speak simply of a 'replica', and allow for *some* physical differences between the dead person and the replica. Badham suggests therefore that the replica would represent the dead person in his normal healthy state rather than in whatever state he was in at the point of death. For this he prefers Dahl's term 'somatic identity' rather than Hick's 'exact replica'. (Despite Hick's own claim that Dahl's view is undeveloped and obscure, Badham believes Hick's view is close to Dahl's.) According to Badham's understanding of Dahl, ' "somatic identity" describes that continu-

[36] *Ibid.*, p. 461. 'We' here means 'everyone'. On Hick's universalism, see below, pp. 128f.
[37] *Christian Beliefs about Life after Death* (London, 1976), pp. 65–84.

ous bodily identity which we recognize our friends as possessing, despite the fact that their constituent parts are in a continuous state of flux. For example, the Bishop of Dorchester is somatically identical with the man who was Principal of Westcott House seven years ago. But he is not materially identical, in that not one cell of his body has remained from his earlier state.'[38] Hick's theory, then, needs modifying to become 'the hypothesis of divine creation in another galaxy of a psycho-physical "replica" somatically identical with the deceased person.'[39]

In Badham's view, this modified theory is intelligible and logically possible. And yet, he insists, a few moments' reflection reveal that the theory has bizarre implications – colonization of innumerable planets and a vast planetary population explosion (since a sexless resurrection would not retain somatic identity). The theory therefore has to be rejected, 'not only because of the immense practical difficulties . . ., but also because it does not seem to be something we might reasonably expect a loving God to bring about.'[40] The criticism seems devastating. But, as one reviewer puts it, 'the *reductio* is fun, the rejection of the heaven of the space-men inevitable – but is it really fair to Hick?'[41] The bizarre details listed by Badham contrast sharply with the proper restraint which characterizes Hick's presentation. In any case, most of the absurdities result from Badham's transference of the 'replica' body from Hick's 'another space' to 'another place' within our space. But his critique of the notion of an '*exact* replica' does expose the weakness of Hick's underplaying of St Paul's emphasis on the resurrection body as a *transformed* body.

Leaving aside such specific aspects of Hick's argument, we may note that his synthesis of eastern and western thought is very speculative. It shows what can emerge when the notion of Jesus and the New Testament as normative revelation of God is abandoned.[42] The scheme of steady progress in various embodiments from death to the ultimate state may sound plausible, even (as Hick claims) on certain Christian presuppositions. But it is very different from the New

---

[38] *Ibid.*, p. 66.   [39] *Ibid.*, p. 78.
[40] *Ibid.*, p. 84.   [41] *ExpT* 88, 1976–77, p. 131.
[42] Hick explains his presuppositions and method of investigation in *Death and Eternal Life*, pp. 22–34. For a statement which seems to make no distinction in status between Jesus and the Buddha, see p. 455.

Testament writers' expectation of the future life as a fulfilled life with Christ in a transformed, glorious environment. And Hick's belief that we must pass through a series of stages towards ultimate fulfilment presupposes an inadequate doctrine of grace. If God is the *giver* of perfection, why should we suppose that the dead must pass through a succession of stages in order to receive it?

Paul Badham: a defence of the concept of the soul

In his survey of *Christian Beliefs about Life after Death* Paul Badham defends the view, stemming from Descartes, that mind (or soul) and brain are correlated but not identical ('Cartesian dualism'), and argues that a concept of soul is required to ensure personal continuity between this life and the next. We cannot base our argument on bodily continuity since the traditional view that our physical body will be literally resurrected is untenable today.

Badham does not, however, dismiss the notion of bodily resurrection, though his own preference seems to be for a disembodied after-life, as we shall see in a moment. But he believes that 're-embodiment in heaven' is logically possible, as long as the resurrection body is conceived of as different from the earthly body (which is the view of most modern theologians). On this view, heaven must be a place, since bodies must live somewhere; and Austin Farrer has shown that one can, on the basis of modern physics, postulate a location for heaven in a different space from ours.[43] Badham insists, however, that since there can be no *material* connection between the earthly body and the resurrection body, personal continuity can be ensured only by a soul.[44]

In discussing the resurrection of Jesus, Badham doubts the reliability of the empty tomb tradition. Rather than thinking of Jesus' resurrection body as his earthly body miraculously transformed, he interprets the resurrection appearances as 'veridical hallucinations' – 'hallucinations' because Jesus was not physically present, 'veridical' because the appearances are related to a real event independent of the percipient's mind. Through the appearances Jesus himself

[43] *Saving Belief* (London, 1964), p. 145.
[44] *Christian Beliefs about Life after Death*, pp. 85–94.

revealed his continued aliveness to his disciples. In other words, Badham is offering a 'theory of Jesus' soul being his true self, continuing to exist after the death of his body, and manifesting his presence to the disciples through a telepathic communication to their minds.'[45] This paves the way for a defence of the concept of a soul, and hence of the view that the future life for *us* is analogous to *Jesus'* victory over death, as defined above.

The concept of the soul and its survival of death has been unpopular in recent years for two main reasons. First, the emphasis in biblical theology on man as a psychosomatic unity seems to relegate the concept of 'soul' to the condemned category of 'Greek thought'. And secondly, the theory of 'mind/brain identity', popularized in Gilbert Ryle's *The Concept of Mind* (London, 1949), has been widely regarded as dealing the death-blow to the concept of 'soul'. This theory holds that there is no 'mind' or 'soul' in man which can be distinguished from the physical body and might therefore survive the body's death. 'Mind' is simply a function of the brain – or, as Cabanis' famous saying crudely puts it, 'the brain secretes thought as the liver secretes bile.'[46]

Badham believes that Ryle's arguments have been successfully refuted by H. D. Lewis in *The Elusive Mind* (London, 1969).[47] Among the points he makes, drawn partly from Lewis, are the following.

a. He is persuaded that telepathy is an empirical fact, and is incompatible with the mind/brain identity theory because it presupposes that information can be transmitted and received by means other than the senses (which is the sphere in which the brain operates).[48]

b. Like any determinist system, the mind/brain identity theory is a self-refuting theory, because if it were true, it would be impossible to establish the validity of any argument. If our minds are physically

---

[45] *Ibid.*, p. 38.

[46] Quoted in R. Aldwinckle, *Death in the Secular City*, p. 71. Incidentally, the theory is not, in essence, new: it was known to Plato (*Phaedo* 86).

[47] See also Lewis' discussion in *Philosophy of Religion* (London, 1965), pp. 273–288; *The Self and Immortality.*

[48] For Badham's discussion of telepathy and his reply to those who accept the reality of telepathy but do not agree that it refutes the identity theory, see *Christian Beliefs about Life after Death*, pp. 113–124.

determined, we have no way of deciding between the merits of different theories of knowledge. Only if we are free agents can we check the validity of our own reasoning: a computer (which in effect is what our minds would be if thought were *merely* a function of brain cells) can calculate many things, but cannot check the validity of its own programming.[49] To these arguments we may add two more from Aldwinckle (who also acknowledges his debt to H. D. Lewis).[50]

c. We all in fact act as though there were an 'I' who is the subject of our bodies' experiences. If there is no such 'I' over and above our bodies, our experience is incoherent. Concepts such as freedom and responsibility become meaningless – for if all the cells in my body are different from seven years ago, why do I feel responsible for what I did seven years ago? This persistent aspect of human experience cannot be lightly dismissed.

d. The scientist studying another human being does not see that person's 'self' or 'soul', but studies only the external, material aspect. We can speak meaningfully about the 'self' only by studying our own selves. The experience of selfhood, of being the 'owners' of our bodies and the subject of our experiences, cannot be dismissed as illusion simply because the scientific method – which operates by observation 'from outside' – cannot cope with it.

I am not sure whether as much can be claimed for telepathy as Badham claims. But the other three arguments are sufficient to show that the concept of soul is defensible, even though it may need pruning of many ideas popularly associated with it.

Badham, then, has argued that it makes sense to say that man has a soul distinguishable from the body – a soul which can therefore ensure personal continuity through death. He goes on to offer a modified form of Price's argument, which we have already examined, to show the possibility of the soul surviving as an experiencing self apart from the body. Badham concludes that Price's theory of a purely mental existence is logically possible and internally coherent. It satisfies the Christian belief in divine justice (since the idea of a life to come shaped out of our desires and our character fits with New Testament teaching that 'we reap what we sow'). It expresses

[49] *Ibid.*, pp. 125–132.
[50] See *Death in the Secular City*, pp. 75–79.

the Christian hope that we may progress toward fullness of life in the world beyond. It allows for social interaction in the future world (through telepathic communication). It coheres with the resurrection appearances of Jesus understood as veridical hallucinations. And it helps to explain the concept of the beatific vision (since an increase in telepathic powers implies also an increase in experience of God).[51]

Badham thus attempts to express Price's theory in terms consistent with Christian tradition. But whilst his exposition is consistent with some strands of biblical teaching and Christian tradition, I question whether it offers a balanced picture of, for example, divine judgment or the heavenly life. The strand of intrinsic self-imposed judgment (which Badham's view implies) is important in the Bible; but if overplayed it can cease to be thought of as *divine* judgment. The heavenly life as conceived by Badham is a far more private life than seems compatible with the New Testament message. And can such a view be expressed in a way that makes it attractive or desirable to ordinary Christians?

John Macquarrie: 'ongoing participation in the life of God'

A different approach has recently been suggested by John Macquarrie.[52] Whilst sympathetic to the notion of a resurrection body, and critical of the doctrine of an immaterial and immortal soul, he proposes to build his view on 'a consideration of the temporality of the self. That is to say, we try to see the self as a pattern in time, just as the body is a pattern disposed in space.'[53] It is characteristic of the human self, he says, to hold together past, present and future in a 'span of time', just as when listening to music we hold in our heads a whole sequence of notes and not just the note which is being played at any one moment. So even in the midst of time we have a taste of eternity. And God's experience, we may suppose, is analogous – in him all time is 'gathered up'. Thus the past which has perished for us is still present in God, and this is how our experience of eternal life after death is to be conceived.

---

[51] *Christian Beliefs about Life after Death*, p. 146.
[52] *Christian Hope* (Oxford, 1978), pp. 117–127; see also *Principles of Christian Theology* (London, ²1977), pp. 357–364; and 'Death and Eternal Life', *ExpT* 89, 1977–78, pp. 46–48.
[53] *Christian Hope*, p. 117.

Macquarrie resists the criticism that he understands eternal life as being *'merely* a static existence' in the memory of God – like a fly caught centuries ago in amber. Rather, it means an ongoing participation in the life of God himself. Each man's past is transformed, in the sense that what has happened in his life comes to take on a new value and to be seen in a new light, even though its 'happenedness' cannot be altered. This is God's reconciling work, which reaches into all time, including the past, and overcomes the poisons of history.

Macquarrie illustrates and supports his argument by means of modern relativity theory. For example, we are familiar with the idea that when we look at a star in the night sky, we are actually seeing it as it was some time ago. Although the whole sky and all the objects in it are simultaneously present to our senses, we are in fact looking over a wide range of times. The concept of an absolute present, and therefore a rigid separation of past and future, has been abolished. And if this is true of our perception and experience, even more must it be true of God. Thus it makes sense to speak of the whole of the past being present for God.

One of Macquarrie's reasons for preferring this approach to the traditional theories of the immortality of the soul and the resurrection of the dead is that it involves us (he argues) in fewer bizarre speculations. If this is a strength, it is also a weakness. For in resisting speculation he leaves some central issues obscure. He does not make clear what he means by 'ongoing participation in the life of God'. I respect his claim that his view is a positive affirmation and not a minimizing view of eternal life. But I remain puzzled as to what this concept of eternal life *means* for the individual in his relationship to Christ and to other individuals who participate in eternal life. Further exposition from Macquarrie and discussion of his theory may clarify it and help us to see whether this 'third approach' is preferable to the two more traditional approaches. But, for the time being, more traditional forms of expression seem more meaningful.

One can only agree, however, with Macquarrie's insistence that, whilst the theologian may make use of the thought of men such as Heidegger or Einstein, 'his belief rests finally on this, that if God is indeed the God of love revealed in Jesus Christ, then death will not

109

wipe out his care for the persons he has created.'[54]

The intermediate state: various opinions

If we affirm belief in life after death, and also in a genuinely future parousia of Jesus, we must find an adequate way of coping with the problem of what happens to persons between their death and the parousia of Christ. This is the problem of the intermediate state, which is in turn connected with the problem of the relation between time and eternity. How can we do justice to the fact that some New Testament texts speak of the believer's being 'with Christ' immediately after death (*e.g.* Lk. 23:43; Phil. 1:23), while others presuppose a general resurrection at the parousia (*e.g.* Jn. 5:28f.; 1 Cor. 15; 1 Thes. 4:16)? We shall look briefly at four solutions.

a. During the interval between death and parousia, the dead are 'with Christ' (Phil. 1:23), but in a disembodied form. Not till the parousia will they, with all other believers, receive their resurrection bodies. This is the view of Cullmann, who emphasizes that this disembodied intermediate state is the subject of Paul's discussion in that much-debated passage, 2 Corinthians 5:1–10. During this intermediate stage, as during earthly life, the Holy Spirit is our guarantee of ultimate resurrection.[55]

This view looks plausible, but if Paul intended to teach the reality of an intermediate state, might we not reasonably expect him to say so more clearly? In the passages cited by advocates of this view there is no indication that this 'being with Christ' is only an interim state before the resurrection. And how is a bodiless 'being with Christ' to be envisaged?

b. Murray Harris argues that from the time he wrote 2 Corinthians 5:1–10 Paul believed the resurrection body to be received at death. The parousia thus became for Paul not the moment of resurrection but the moment of open manifestation of a previously hidden state of embodiment.[56] Thus there is still an intermediate

---

[54] *Ibid.*, p. 127.

[55] *Christ and Time*, pp. 238–242. For a similar view, see G. C. Berkouwer, *The Return of Christ*, pp. 32–64. There is a survey of recent interpretations of 2 Cor. 5:1–10 in F. G. Lang, *2 Kor. 5:1–10 in den neueren Forschung* (Tübingen, 1973) and a bibliography in F. F. Bruce, *1 and 2 Corinthians* (London, 1971) p. 201.

[56] '2 Corinthians 5:1–10: Watershed in Paul's Eschatology?', *TynB* 22, 1971, pp. 32–57. The same view is held by F. F. Bruce, 'Paul on Immortality', *SJT* 24, 1971, pp. 457–472.

state, but not an awkwardly disembodied one. Harris has made a strong case for his interpretation of 2 Corinthians 5, but C. K. Barrett in his 1973 commentary is not impressed with the view that 2 Corinthians 5 represents a development from the position in 1 Corinthians 15 that the resurrection body will be received at the parousia.[57] And in a later letter (Phil. 3:20f.) Paul seems to associate resurrection with the parousia.

Aldwinckle also believes that the intermediate state will involve an embodied existence: 'the idea of being in Christ as only half a person does not make sense.'[58] In that case the general resurrection at the parousia would denote not our passing from a disembodied to an embodied state, but our entry into full communion with the whole body of the faithful.

c. The doctrine of 'soul-sleep' holds that there is a time-interval for the dead person between his death and the general resurrection, but that he spends it 'sleeping', unconscious. It was the view of 'Psychopannychians' in the Middle Ages, of some Anabaptists at the Reformation; and Luther was suspected of it, though his position appears to have been closer to the fourth view summarized below. Today it is the position of Seventh Day Adventists and Jehovah's Witnesses, and of some who are closer to an orthodox Christian standpoint. It is difficult to see how such a view is to be reconciled with the vivid hope of Philippians 1:23. It leans far too heavily on the New Testament's occasional use of 'sleep' as a metaphor for death.[59]

d. Others argue that time is an entity belonging to this world; it is part of the created order, having no absolute significance. Therefore, whatever may happen to persons after death, we have no reason to assume that they remain within our space-time system. Thus, T. F. Torrance is able to suggest that when the believer dies he goes to

---

[57] *A Commentary on the Second Epistle to the Corinthians* (London, 1973), pp. 150–161.
[58] *Death in the Secular City*, p. 144.
[59] The doctrine is discussed and rejected by G. C. Berkouwer, *The Return of Christ*, pp. 59–61; and L. Boettner, *Immortality* (London, 1956), pp. 108–117. That Luther, despite his frequent use of the image of sleep, did not hold this doctrine seems clear in the light of his view that time is inapplicable beyond death – see T. F. Torrance, *Kingdom and Church* (Edinburgh-London, 1956), pp. 9,19. Cullmann also has been thought to teach 'soul-sleep' in *Immortality of the Soul or Resurrection of the Dead?*, pp. 48–57; but since he uses the word 'sleep' there in inverted commas without defining it, except to say that those who 'sleep' are close to Christ and controlled by the Holy Spirit, it seems more accurate to include him under view *a*.

be with Christ (*cf.* Phil. 1:23) and receives his resurrection body. From *his* perspective there is no gap between his death and Christ's parousia. But from the perspective of those who live on in time, there is an interval between his death and the parousia – hence the texts which speak of a still future general resurrection. The whole problem of the intermediate state arises because people insist on viewing the state of the dead from the perspective of our time-bound existence, but it is idle to assume that the dead would wish to be so limited![60] This last view – that from the viewpoint of the dead themselves there is no 'intermediate state' – seems to me to involve the fewest difficulties.

A possible Christian perspective on the future life

Much of this chapter has discussed life after death in terms of what is plausible or logically possible. Such excursions into philosophy are important, because – as H. D. Lewis says – 'unless certain views about the nature of persons can be sustained and others rebutted, it is idle to embark on any consideration of life after death'. Yet it is in 'the *religious* context . . ., rather than in general metaphysical arguments, that we can find the strongest and most enduring support for the view that this life is not all'.[61] For Christians it is their experience and understanding of *God* which both makes life after death believable and suggests what form that life may take. This was the argument of Jesus in his reply to the Sadducees – '. . . I am the God of Abraham, and the God of Isaac, and the God of Jacob. . . .' (Mk. 12:26). Baillie commented: 'The argument is unanswerable; and is indeed the only unanswerable argument for immortality that has ever been given, or ever can be given. It cannot be evaded except by a denial of the premises. If the individual can commune with God, then he must matter to God; and if he matters to God, he must share God's eternity. For if God really rules, he cannot be conceived as scrapping what is precious in his sight. It is in the conjunction with God that the promise of eternal life resides.'[62] The

---

[60] T. F. Torrance, *Space, Time and Resurrection* (Edinburgh, 1976), p. 102. See also the discussion in H. Schwarz, *On the Way to the Future* (Minneapolis, 1972), pp. 185–193.

[61] *The Self and Immortality*, p. 205. *Cf.* Sutherland, *Religious Studies* 3, 1967–68, pp. 388f.

[62] *And the Life Everlasting*, p. 137. There are similar statements in D. H. van Daalen, *The Real Resurrection* (London, 1972), p. 164; H. D. Lewis, *Philosophy of Religion*, pp. 319f.; and

view of Hick, that a life after death is required in order to make sense of life, has already been quoted.[63] It has now emerged that belief in the God disclosed in Christ would be unthinkable without belief in an after-life.

It is in this context that the resurrection of Jesus should be understood. Apart from belief in God, the empty tomb and resurrection appearances would be strange, inexplicable phenomena. But if *God* raised Jesus from the dead (as the New Testament writers persistently affirm), then the resurrection falls into place as 'a mighty act of the living God . . ., pivotal in the whole scheme of man's salvation.'[64]

Willi Marxsen is right to stress that the resurrection appearances are not the same as the resurrection itself, but wrong to claim that 'resurrection' is only an interpretation, 'an inference derived from personal faith'.[65] Something had to happen to create this faith. Whether or not the disciples accepted current apocalyptic expectations of the resurrection of the dead, there was no precedent for their conviction that already *within history* a resurrection had taken place which anticipated the general resurrection at the end of history.[66] The empty tomb tradition, which (for reasons such as those given by C. F. D. Moule[67]) I believe to be early and reliable, does not prove the resurrection, but witnesses to the nature of the resurrection. For it indicates that through the resurrection the body of Jesus was somehow transformed into a new mode of existence – the glorified existence of the age to come.[68]

But what is the connection between Jesus' resurrection and the resurrection of other men? J. A. T. Robinson asserts: 'Nowhere in the New Testament is the resurrection hope deduced from the

---

the argument from God's character and purpose (as revealed in Christ) is the central argument of M. Perry, *The Resurrection of Man* (see especially pp. 48–72).

[63] Above, p. 99; *cf*; S. W. Sykes in *Creation, Christ and Culture*, pp. 260–262.

[64] M. Perry, *The Resurrection of Man*, p. 49.

[65] *The Resurrection of Jesus of Nazareth* (London, 1970), p. 138.

[66] J. Jeremias, *New Testament Theology*, 1 (London, 1971), pp. 308f.; C. F. Evans, *Resurrection and the New Testament* (London, 1970), pp. 39f.

[67] C. F. D. Moule (ed.), *The Significance of the Message of the Resurrection for Faith in Jesus Christ* (London, 1968), pp. 8f.; *cf*. J. A. T. Robinson in *Interpreter's Dictionary of the Bible*, 3, pp. 45–47. The opposite view is argued by Lampe in G. W. H. Lampe and D. M. Mackinnon, *The Resurrection* (London, 1966), pp. 41–58.

[68] For an excellent conservative discussion of the nature of the resurrection, see G. E. Ladd, *I Believe in the Resurrection of Jesus* (London, 1975).

resurrection of Christ, as if his survival of death were the supreme instance that proved or guaranteed eternal life for others.'[69] Strictly speaking, this may be true: as we have seen, Jesus himself based his belief in resurrection on his conviction about God, and there is a sense in which Jesus' resurrection *presupposes* a general resurrection (1 Cor. 15:16). But Robinson's statement gives a misleadingly negative impression. For the New Testament writers constantly assert that in Jesus' resurrection God has demonstrated his purpose of raising other men in the future, and that it is through union with Christ that this resurrection becomes possible for men. This intimate link between Christ's resurrection and ours is indicated, for example, in John 11:25f.; Romans 6:5; 8:29; 1 Corinthians 15:20–23; 1 Peter 1:3f.

The resurrection of Jesus gives some clues not only about the fact of our resurrection but also about its nature. Paul, indeed, regarded the risen body of Christ as a 'model' for our resurrection bodies. This idea seems to underlie his whole argument in 1 Corinthians 15 (*cf.* the 'first fruits' metaphor in verses 20, 23), and is expressed in Philippians 3:21. But this gives rise to a problem. I have already suggested, on the basis of the empty tomb stories, that Jesus' physical body was raised and transformed into a new mode of existence. But clearly that process cannot happen to us, whose bodies disintegrate in the tomb. So the resurrection of men cannot follow exactly the pattern of Jesus' resurrection. To be sure, one of Lampe's main reasons for believing that Jesus' tomb was not empty is his desire to avoid the inference that Jesus' resurrection was in any way different from the resurrection of other men.[70] Yet there is no *a priori* reason for deducing this specific point from the general principle that Christ must in every respect share our human nature: it is not normally deduced, for example, that because Jesus shared our human lot he was therefore sinful. So it is not self-evident that our resurrection should be exactly like Jesus' – in any case, Jesus' resurrection is unique in that it occurred within history, as an anticipation of other resurrections.

In his description of the resurrection body (1 Cor. 15:35–58) Paul insists both on the continuity between the present material body and

---

[69] *Interpreter's Dictionary of the Bible*, 3, p. 45.   [70] *The Resurrection*, pp. 58f.

the resurrection body (NB the 'it' which remains the subject right through verses 42–44) and on the discontinuity (*e.g.*, in the contrasts of verses 42–44). The seed metaphor quite naturally suggests both continuity and discontinuity.[71] But unless we can find a way of suggesting how our physical bodies might be reconstituted after death, it seems impossible to accept that there is material continuity between this life and the next. There may – indeed there must – be continuity of person, or self, or soul. But there will be discontinuity of body. That there will be a resurrection *body* is stressed in 1 Corinthians 15, and embodiment seems (at least from our present perspective) necessary to facilitate self-expression, communication and personal relationships in the resurrection world. But we cannot say what form the resurrection body will take. We might opt for Hick's 'exact replica in another space', or we might be more agnostic and be content with Paul's description of it as imperishable, glorious, spiritual (1 Cor. 15:42–44, where 'spiritual' means not 'non-material' but 'controlled by the Holy Spirit').

Does such a view satisfy the philosopher's requirements for safeguarding the continuity of personal identity through death? The three strands of continuity normally invoked are memory, bodily identity and the continuity of character or mental characteristics. Yet we do not always require all three strands to convince ourselves of a person's identity. If, for example, a person suffers brain damage in an accident and thereby loses all memory of his former life and becomes changed in character, his physical identity through this experience is sufficient to persuade us that he is still the same person. Now, if I am resurrected, I presumably retain memory of my former life, and some at least of my personal characteristics. The concept of the soul, as defended by Badham, would ensure that. The fact that I no longer have the same body is not sufficient to rule out real continuity. But is the continuity not ruled out by the fact that my resurrection takes place long after my death, so that there is an unbridgeable gulf, a fatal gap in my memory? No, for what is

[71] The continuity is stressed by R. H. Gundry, *Sōma in Biblical Theology*, pp. 161–183; J. S. Schep, *The Nature of the Resurrection Body* (Grand Rapids, 1964); R. J. Sider, 'The Pauline Conception of the Resurrection Body in 1 Cor. 15:35–54', *NTS* 21, 1974–75, pp. 428–439. For examples of those who stress discontinuity see M. E. Dahl, *The Resurrection of the Body*, pp. 11–19.

important about memory is not that I can remember everything that has ever happened to me without a break, but that I can remember *some* things from my past. Today I have no means of remembering what happened while I was asleep last night, but I can remember what happened yesterday. And I recall experiences of three or thirty years ago, and recognize myself as the subject of those experiences. One could also argue that, if I was right to suggest that at death we pass beyond this earthly time-series, it is not a matter of resurrection 'long after' death; from the viewpoint of the person who dies, resurrection is instantaneous.[72]

In the context of thinking about the continuity problem, it is worth observing how 1 Corinthians 15 has dominated all discussion of New Testament teaching on resurrection, to the neglect of passages affirming the believer's present relationship with Christ which continues through death to the resurrection world – *e.g.*, John 3:36; 5:24; Romans 8:11; 2 Corinthians 4:16.

Whatever view we adopt of the 'intermediate state', we should recognize that the New Testament writers' insistence on a resurrection at the parousia indicates the *corporate* nature of salvation. In a sense, no one will be saved until all are saved. The idea of an individualized immortality attained at death – with nothing further to follow – fails to reflect the Christian insight that true life is always life-in-community.

The resurrection world will be in a space other than ours, as Farrer has suggested.[73] And since the life of that world will be a consummation of our present experience of God, we may envisage it as a fuller experience of our present 'relationship to God, our dependence upon him, the enjoyment of fellowship with him, the social bonds of love which unite all who are in Christ.'[74] There will be growth in (rather than towards) the good. And if the experiences and activities implied thereby can only be envisaged as taking place in some form of 'succession' or 'time', so be it. But that need not mean the same

---

[72] On the question whether continuity of personal identity is threatened by the attaining of moral perfection instantaneously at the resurrection, see below, p. 131.

[73] Above, n. 11. Karl Heim has also thought in terms of 'another dimension', in his books which attempt to relate Christian faith to modern physics, *e.g.*, *The Christian Faith and Natural Science* (ET, London, 1953), pp. 126–150; *The World: its Creation and Consummation* (ET, Edinburgh-London, 1962), pp. 137–139.

[74] R. Aldwinckle, *Death in the Secular City*, p. 168.

time as our present time.

A further clue to the nature of the resurrection world is suggested by Christ's resurrection. Just as his earthly body was somehow 'used up' in the transformation to his new mode of existence, so all worthwhile activity and creativity will be taken up from this world into the world to come. Nothing is wasted (*cf.* the clues of 1 Cor. 15:58; Rev. 21:26).[75] How this would work out in practice, we can only imagine. But if we are entitled to draw clues about the life to come from the Christian understanding of God, we may agree with Aldwinckle: 'We may see in a glass, darkly, . . . but it was surely never the intention of St. Paul to suggest that we can see nothing at all.'[76]

---

[75] This idea is expounded in H. A. Williams, *Jesus and the Resurrection* (London, 1951), pp. 59ff.; and by G. B. Caird, 'The Christological Basis of Christian Hope', in *The Christian Hope*, by Caird *et al.* (London, 1970), pp. 22–24.

[76] *Death in the Secular City*, p. 171.

Chapter Seven

The judgment of God and the future of men

We have seen that the life after death is not something natural and inevitable for man, but something which God gives. But to whom does he give it? To all men, or only to some? Traditionally, most Christians have affirmed belief that Christ will come 'to judge the living and the dead'. The image of the Great Assize with God (or Christ) on his judgment throne, has controlled the imaginations of the faithful, and to some extent their morals. On the day of judgment God would usher men into eternal salvation, or into eternal condemnation. Around the doctrine there gathered various associated ideas and images, of varying degrees of orthodoxy. But in essence the doctrine was defended on the grounds that it was biblical, and that simple justice demanded it. In recent years very few theologians have expounded and defended this traditional approach, though there have been a few fine studies of the biblical material.[1] There have, however, been several significant expositions of the view, known as universalism, that all men will ultimately enjoy eternal life in the resurrection world. The main purpose of this chapter will be to evaluate the various views on whether salvation will be experienced by all men or only by some, and to suggest a coherent understanding of divine judgment. But first a brief reference must be made to one aspect of divine judgment as understood by Roman Catholics, namely the doctrine of purgatory.

[1] *E.g.*, A. T. Hanson, *The Wrath of the Lamb* (London, 1957); J. A. Baird, *The Justice of God in the Teaching of Jesus* (London, 1963); a briefer survey is L. Morris, *The Biblical Doctrine of Judgment* (London, 1960). The development away from traditional doctrines during the seventeenth and nineteenth centuries respectively, is charted by D. P. Walker, *The Decline of Hell* (London, 1964); G. Rowell, *Hell and the Victorians* (Oxford, 1974).

Purgatory

The core of the doctrine is that between the individual's death and the general resurrection there is a purification for all who 'died truly penitent in the love of God before making satisfaction for their sins through worthy fruits of penance'.[2] It is thus experienced by people whose ultimate destiny has already been determined at death. It is felt to reflect the conviction that human beings can attain their complete fulfilment only gradually, and that suffering is a normal element in personal growth.[3] The doctrine is associated with prayer for the dead (*cf.* 2 Macc. 12:39–45), which is believed to hasten this process of growth through suffering.

The doctrine may be criticised because it is lacking in biblical evidence. It undermines the effectiveness of God's grace by denying God's full acceptance of believers in Christ. It contradicts the New Testament's emphasis that the after-life will be quite different from this life: for the idea of praying for the dead presupposes a similarity between this life and the next. And how, in any case, are we to conceive of growth taking place in bodiless souls (which those in purgatory are presumed to be)? Curiously, two significant changes have happened to the doctrine of purgatory in recent years. First, Roman Catholic writers have largely ceased to use supposed scriptural evidence (*e.g.,* 1 Cor. 3:15) to defend the doctrine, and have appealed more to the Fathers (see, *e.g.,* Tertullian, *On Monogamy* 10; Augustine, *Confessions* 11:11). Secondly, a concept of purgatory has been accepted by many Protestant theologians who write about the after-life (as we shall see below).

A variation on traditional teaching about purgatory is suggested by the Jesuit, Ladislaus Boros. He advocates the theory of a final decision made for or against Christ when men come into the presence of God at the moment of death. 'Purgatory would be the passage, which we effect in our final decision, through the purifying fire of divine love. The encounter with Christ would be our purgatory.'[4] The idea is attractive but speculative; and it is not clear why it should be equated with purgatory.[5]

---

[2] See *Sacramentum Mundi* 5, p. 167.
[3] See R. Gleason, *The World to Come* (London, 1959), pp. 101–103.
[4] *The Moment of Truth* (ET, London, 1965), p. 139.
[5] *Cf.* the comments of M. Paternoster, *Thou Art There Also* (London, 1967), pp. 126f. (This

The love of God and his judgment of men

I propose now to outline an understanding of divine judgment which is, I believe, consistent with New Testament teaching as mainstream Christianity has interpreted it. If we begin from the fundamental truth that 'God is love', the following corollaries emerge.

a. Because God knows and loves every human individual, he treats the actions of each as significant. The notion that all men will 'give account' to God affirms and safeguards this truth, and is therefore to be welcomed rather than feared or ignored. If the idea of human responsibility to God is removed, then ultimately no actions are significant.

b. Since love never forces itself on its object, God's love for men implies that he gives us genuine freedom to accept or to reject his love. Hence when God judges a man, the outcome may be either positive or negative, according to whether the man has reacted positively or negatively to God's love. The real possibility of condemnation by God cannot be denied without at the same time denying the reality of human freedom. It is God's respect for human freedom which makes 'hell' possible. If it be objected that that would be a defeat for God, we should consider C. S. Lewis' reply: 'What you call defeat, I call miracle: for to make things which are not Itself, and thus to become, in a sense, capable of being resisted by its own handiwork, is the most astounding and unimaginable of all the feats we attribute to the Deity.'[6]

c. Salvation and condemnation are to be understood primarily in terms of relationship or non-relationship to God through Christ. This is true both of the *criterion* by which judgment is made, and of the *result* of the judgment.

The *criterion* by which men's destinies will be determined is their attitude to Christ – their relationship with him. This is implied in the term 'faith', which involves 'commitment' to someone in relationship. And on the negative side, Paul speaks in 2 Thessalonians 1:8 of 'those who do not know God and do not obey the gospel of

---

is a valuable survey of issues related to judgment and the after-life, with some historical material of the kind covered more fully by Walker and Rowell.

[6] *The Problem of Pain* (London, 1940), p. 115. *Cf.* Rowley, *The Relevance of Apocalyptic* (London, ³1963), pp. 190f.; R. Aldwinckle, *Death in the Secular City* (London, 1972), p. 114.

our Lord Jesus' – they are not in relationship with him, and so will come under his wrath. The factor which will determine men's destiny at the final judgment will be whether or not they are in a loving, responsible relationship to Jesus Christ. This does not contradict the frequent New Testament insistence on 'judgment according to works', since in the New Testament – especially in Paul – works are regarded as evidence of the reality (or otherwise) of the relationship.[7]

The *result* of divine judgment is also to be conceived in terms of relationship to God or to Christ. In his important study of *Jesus and the Future Life* (London, [2]1970), William Strawson says of Matthew 25:31–46 that in the command 'Depart from me' and the invitation 'Come', 'we have in essence what is meant by hell and heaven. To be in hell is to be sent out from the presence of God. . . . Equally, there is no description of heaven more significant than that which is involved in the one word "Come"; for to be with God is to be indeed in heaven.'[8]

This emphasis on *relationship* enables us to understand the link between judgment as a present reality (*cf.*, *e.g.*, Jn. 3:17–21; Rom. 1:18–32) and judgment at the last day. The final judgment means God's underlining and ratification of the relationship or non-relationship with him which men have chosen in this life. If they have fellowship with God now, they will enter into a fuller experience of his presence then. If they do not know him now, they will not know him then.

If this is so, we can see that both heaven and hell are best thought of not as reward or punishment for the kind of life we have lived, but as the logical outcome of our relationship to God in this life. Heaven is not a reward for loving God any more than marriage is a reward for being engaged. And hell is not a punishment for turning one's back on Christ and choosing the road that leads to destruction. It is where the road goes.[9]

If judgment is something which goes on in the present life, and is self-imposed in the sense that we receive what we choose (as in Jn. 3:17–21; Gal. 6:8), what is the point of continuing to speak of a 'last

[7] See *e.g.*, the discussion of Rom. 2:1–11 in L. Mattern, *Der Verständnis des Gerichtes bei Paulus* (Zürich, 1966), pp. 123–140.

[8] *Jesus and the Future Life* (London, [2]1970), p. 126. *Cf.* J. A. Baird, *The Justice of God in the Teaching of Jesus*, pp. 209–227.

[9] *Cf.* A. Farrer, *Saving Belief* (London, 1964), pp. 135–137.

judgment' at the parousia? We may mention two reasons. First, there is a basic distinction between the present judgment and the final judgment, in that the present judgment *is not final*. Men experience God-lessness, with all its implications, only so long as they resist God's love: while life continues, they can change sides. But the last judgment *is final*; the New Testament gives no hint that the verdict is reversible after death. Secondly, the image of the great assize does emphasize certain important truths: judgment is an act of God, not merely an impersonal process; it is serious, it is just, it is inescapable. D. M. Mackinnon comments: 'The ancient theological symbol of the great "assize" has somehow conveyed to generations that God in his omniscience cannot forget; and if that symbol has lost its power for us . . ., we are, perhaps, impoverished by the loss.'[10]

This tension in the New Testament between present and final judgment leads to ambiguity over whether the resurrection will be a resurrection of all men or of believers only. Paul in his letters (*e.g.*, 1 Cor. 15) seems to reserve the term 'resurrection' for the glorified state of believers, and says nothing about a resurrection of unbelievers. Other passages, however, suggest that universal judgment requires a universal resurrection – a 'resurrection of life' and a 'resurrection of judgment' (Jn. 5:29; *cf.* Acts 24:15).[11] But precisely how it will happen is not important: what matters is that we take seriously the truths which such language embodies.

d. Since judgment is a corollary of God's love, C. H. Dodd and A. T. Hanson are wrong to think of the 'wrath' of God as an impersonal 'inevitable process of cause and effect in a moral universe'.[12] Admittedly, the New Testament writers (Paul and John in particular) often speak of judgment as a process whereby people experience the inherent results of the choices they make (Jn. 3:17–21; Rom. 1: 18–32; Gal. 6:8 are perhaps the clearest of many examples).

[10] 'Subjective and Objective Conceptions of Atonement', in F. G. Healey (ed.), *Prospect for Theology: Essays in Honour of H. H. Farmer* (London, 1967), p. 178.

[11] Some have seen a reference to a resurrection of unbelievers in the *telos* of 1 Cor. 15:24; but this view is to be rejected: see C. K. Barrett, *The First Epistle to the Corinthians* (London, 1968), p. 356. But Paul certainly assumed a universal *judgment* (Rom. 2:16; 1 Thes. 1:9f.).

[12] C. H. Dodd, *The Epistle of Paul to the Romans* (London, 1932), p. 23. This well-known view is followed (though with significant variations, and in a survey of the whole Bible) by A. T. Hanson, *The Wrath of the Lamb*.

And nowhere do New Testament writers speak of God as 'being angry' – the noun 'wrath' or 'anger' (*orgē*) has become for them a technical term for God's *action* in judgment (rather than his attitude) and for the lost condition of men. Yet this does not mean that 'wrath' should be described as impersonal. In a divinely controlled universe, if men sin and evil consequences follow, that can only be because God has willed it so. Judgment is a process in which God is involved. For example, in Romans 1:18–32, the *locus classicus* for Dodd's 'impersonal' view, it is three times said that '*God* gave them up . . .' (verses 24, 26, 28); and there is explicit reference to *God's* wrath (verse 18) and *God's* decree (verse 32). I am more in agreement with Dodd's and Hanson's interpretation of God's 'wrath' than my dissent over this personal/impersonal issue might suggest. But I believe that to speak of judgment as 'impersonal' is misleading, and risks distorting the relationship between love and judgment in God. God's wrath, says James Stewart, is his love in agony, 'smitten with dreadful sorrow'.[13]

e. The love of God must govern our handling of the questions that remain once the New Testament's basic perspective has been expounded. What about those who have never heard the gospel adequately presented? What about sincere adherents of non-Christian religions? What about the mentally ill, the socially deprived, those who die young? All such persons must be entrusted to the love of God, in the confidence that he will not deal with them arbitrarily, or in any way which is inconsistent with his love. We must frankly admit that the New Testament gives no explicit answers, and hardly any clues, to such problems. Jesus refused to speculate about whether 'those who are saved will be few', but urged his questioners to 'strive to enter' (Lk. 13:23f.). A theological question is countered with a personal demand.[14]

It is inevitable that we should reflect on questions about the destiny of those who fail to respond in this life to God's love. Yet it seems more honest to confess considerable agnosticism and to insist that judgment is God's function and not ours, than to argue

---

[13] *A Man in Christ* (London, 1935), p. 221. I have expounded in detail my understanding of 'wrath' in Paul in my 1970 Cambridge PhD thesis, *Divine Retribution in the Thought of Paul*.

[14] *Cf.* Strawson's observation that Jesus' warnings about 'Gehenna' always concern the person addressed; they never concern some hypothetical 'others' (*Jesus and the Future Life*, p. 141).

that universal salvation is the only conceivable solution to the problem. To the arguments for universal salvation we now turn.

The case for universalism

The idea that all men will ultimately find salvation was suggested, as is well known, by Origen.[15] Since its advocacy in modern times by Friedrich Schleiermacher, it has steadily gained support.[16] Several factors (apart from emotional or sentimental ones) have caused an increasing number of scholars to opt for some doctrine of universal salvation. The growth of historical criticism of the Gospels, whereby it is believed possible to eliminate some strands of Gospel teaching as not authentic to Jesus, has enabled some to suggest that warnings of divine condemnation derive not from Jesus but from the early church. Similarly, the recognition of mythological elements in the New Testament has facilitated a greater flexibility in interpretation of seemingly 'awkward' texts. Scholars have felt themselves delivered from a former generation's unsophisticated formulation of the view that 'God is love, but his justice demands that he punish those who resist his will'. The belief that some, or most, of mankind will suffer in everlasting torment has been felt by many to be both philosophically and theologically intolerable. And then there is the pressure of the great world religions. In India, for example, there is nearly one sixth of the world's population, but only about 3% profess Christianity: what place do the 500,000,000 Hindus and 70,000,000 Muslims – and smaller numbers of Sikhs, Jains, Buddhists and animists – have in God's purpose?[17] With issues such as these in the background, universalism has become an important topic of theological debate.[18]

---

[15] In De Principiis; see J. N. D. Kelly, Early Christian Doctrines (London, [4]1968), pp. 473f.

[16] Schleiermacher, The Christian Faith (ET, Edinburgh, 1928), pp. 720–722. The original German edition appeared in 1821–2.

[17] For a sensitive treatment of this issue by progressive Roman Catholics (including Hans Küng and Raymond Panikkar), see J. Neuner (ed.), Christian Revelation and World Religions (London, 1967). The book resulted from a conference of Roman Catholic theologians in Bombay in 1964, which concluded, e.g., that men can be saved 'in their own non-Christian religions', which are 'the historical way to God for their followers' (pp. 22, 23).

[18] A useful survey-article is T. F. Glasson, 'Human Destiny: Has Christian Teaching Changed?' Modern Churchman 12, 1969, pp. 284–298. See also R. J. Bauckham, 'Universalism: a Historical Survey', Themelios 4.2, January, 1979, pp. 48–54. Other articles in the same issue criticize universalism from various angles.

In 1934 John Baillie wrote: 'If we decide for universalism, it must be for a form of it which does nothing to decrease the urgency of immediate repentance and which makes no promises to the procrastinating sinner. It is doubtful whether such a form of the doctrine has yet been found. But one has the feeling that in this whole question of the fate of the unrepentant we are touching one of the growing-points of Christian thought at the present time.'[19] Several expositions of universalism in recent years have avoided the risk of basing the hope of universal salvation simply on a shallow optimism, and have grappled seriously with the tension between God's love and human freedom, between the gravity of sin and God's power to forgive and transform. We shall consider them in (more or less) chronological order.

C. F. D. Moule, in *The Meaning of Hope* (London, 1953) faced the question whether 'God's purposes of love have not been defeated when nine-tenths of his creation disown him. . . .?' His reply is that man's free will to reject God must be affirmed with utter seriousness – and yet it seems impossible to believe that such infinitely patient love as God shows in Christ can ultimately be defeated. Both sides of the paradox must be held. There is the urgency of decision – and yet the conviction that 'if *we* cannot rest without knowing that our loved ones are right with God, is it conceivable that *God* can be content to let them go?' He then uses the biblical image of 'firstfruits' to develop the idea that the church represents but the first instalment of God's universal saving purpose. But he leaves his suggestions comparatively undeveloped, being content to reflect the New Testament's own reticence about details of 'the beyond'.[20] The very simplicity of his statement has a persuasiveness which is not found in many expressions of universalism.

A more developed and more subtle presentation of a similar approach is J. A. T. Robinson's *In the End God*.[21] Robinson observes that in the New Testament there are two pictures of the end which are in tension with each other: some texts speak of a universal restoration of all things (*e.g.*, 1 Cor. 15:24–28), while

---

[19] *And the Life Everlasting* (London, 1934), p. 245.

[20] *The Meaning of Hope*, pp. 48–56.

[21] The original edition of course appeared in 1950, before Moule's book; I refer to the revised edition of 1968, where the issue is discussed on pp. 110–133.

others insist on judgment and separation between the saved and the lost (*e.g.*, Mt. 25: 31–46). These are not literal predictions, of which one must be true and the other false, but 'myths', both of which represent 'elements in the total Christian understanding of the End which must be retained together.'[22]

Resisting other solutions to the dilemma, Robinson stresses that if God is ultimately to be 'all in all', all men must ultimately be saved. If a human being had the power to resist God's love for ever, 'this power would have shown itself to be stronger than God and thereby have reared a final disproof of the omnipotence of his love.' In that case, 'God would simply cease to be God.'[23] He would certainly not be the God who revealed himself through his work in Christ.

Yet, says Robinson, we must do justice equally to the myth of final judgment, with its emphasis on the reality of human freedom, and the seriousness of hell. He observes that on the human level, when another's love draws a response from us, we do not feel that our freedom has been destroyed: we *can* choose to remain unmoved. May we not then imagine a love so strong – God's love – 'that ultimately no one will be able to restrain himself from free and grateful surrender?'[24] That at least will suggest to us that all *could* be saved. We can go on to assert that all *will* be saved because our personal experience of God persuades us that 'the power of *this* love could experience no bounds at all, and that even our desire that it should not conquer us completely will be taken from our willing hearts. This strange contradiction will irritate the philosopher, but the person in actual gracious relation to God knows from experience that the necessary victory of God's love would not abrogate, but simply release, our freedom.'[25]

As for 'the reality of hell', the myth of the last judgment emphasizes the unlimited implications of decision for or against God: to the man in decision, hell is as real a destination as heaven. As long as he chooses death, he is choosing irreversible and eternal death. The believer knows that God must win all men. But it is fatal to transfer that confidence, which is valid only for the subject 'in the truth', to

[22] *In the End God*, p. 111.   [23] *Ibid.*, p. 118.
[24] *Ibid.*, p. 122.   [25] *Ibid.*, p. 125.

make it hold 'objectively' apart from faith. For that would take the edge off all moral seriousness. But *in the end*, 'in a universe of love there can be no heaven which tolerates a chamber of horrors, no hell for any which does not at the same time make it hell for God.'[26]

Michael Paternoster, feeling that Robinson's view involves him in self-contradiction and that his 'use of the concept of "myth" leaves one unclear about fact', offers a 'more prosaic and less profound' view. He suggests that 'universalism must be true if God is God; but that hell is a fact of *present* experience.'[27] People experience hell – alienation from God – in terms of loneliness, loss of identity and lack of purpose. But God is ceaselessly active, seeking to draw us to himself. And there is no reason to believe that this process will cease at our death. 'Since God does not change, his methods cannot, and in any future world he must proceed as he does in this, to train men gradually and patiently to take their proper place in the scheme of things. A process incomplete at the time of death must be completed elsewhere.'[28] The denial of the eternity of hell does not remove the urgency of responding to the gospel, for all men are in hell as long as they resist God's love. But as soon as they learn to accept their sufferings as God's means of bringing them to himself, their hell is turned into purgatory, and they are on the way towards their ultimate goal, the vision of God.

Michael Perry, who also believes that people's attitudes towards God may be transformed by a gradual 'purgatorial' process after death, uses the analogy of a sherry party. The party is meant to be an enjoyable affair, but it may feel like 'hell' for someone who does not know any of the other guests and knows nothing about their topics of conversation. So with the life to come, those who have prepared themselves for it by cultivating the presence of God and obeying his will are likely to feel at ease. But the man who has had no time for God will find that what is heaven for the person who loves God is hell for him. He will be uncomfortable in God's presence – 'in the party but out of the swim'.[29] But God cannot leave him uncomfortable. 'The only solution worthy of the name of Christian is the one which leads us to affirm that in the end all men will

[26] *Ibid.*, p. 133.　[27] *Thou Art There Also*, p. 141.
[28] *Ibid.*, p. 151.　[29] *The Resurrection of Man*, p. 90.

be saved and will come to the knowledge and enjoyment of God's love. . . . If this leads us to difficulties when seen in the light of other doctrines, then it is the other doctrines which need modification. Christ is the second Adam, not the second Noah; he will redeem all mankind, not the righteous only.'[30]

So, like Paternoster, Perry is saying that hell is real – for a time. A man does not experience redemption without wanting it: but God's love, sooner or later, will cause him to want it.

The final presentation of universalism which we shall consider is John Hick's. In *Evil and the God of Love* he argues that 'God will eventually succeed in his purpose of winning all men to himself in faith and love.'[31] We must, he suggests, distinguish between the logical and factual questions involved. Logically, it is contradictory to say that creatures endowed with free will are predetermined ultimately to love God. But factually, God – the nature of whose love we experience in the present – will surely persist, like a divine psychotherapist, in helping his patients to find their true selves. In theory he could fail; but it is a practical certainty that in the end he will succeed. We must take seriously Jesus' warnings that selfish deeds lead to real sufferings after death, but must believe that because God is love those sufferings will be temporal and redemptive. Thus Hick summarizes the thesis of his book: 'God has ordained a world which contains evil – real evil – as a means to the creation of the infinite good of a kingdom of Heaven within which his creatures will have come as perfected persons to love and serve him, through a process in which their own free insight and response have been an essential element.'[32]

In *Death and Eternal Life* Hick develops this argument.[33] In considering the New Testament evidence, he accepts that in a few Synoptic passages (Mt. 25:31–46; probably Mt. 25:30; Mk. 3:29) *eternal* torment seems to be taught. But there are many other passages referring to judgment which do not specify that condemnation is eternal. Why, asks Hick, should the larger number of references be interpreted in the light of the smaller? Again, it is true that the Fourth Gospel speaks of two 'races' of people, with two destinies

---

[30] *Ibid.*, p. 91.   [31] *Evil and the God of Love* (London, [2]1977), p. 342.
[32] *Ibid.*, p. 363.   [33] *Death and Eternal Life* (London, 1976), pp. 242–261.

only. But the doctrine of predestination underlying this view is as unacceptable to the modern non-universalist as to the universalist; and a system which offers only two outcomes – death or life – is ethically intolerable. Moreover, alongside these 'judgment' passages we must set the 'universalist' passages where Paul, driven by the logic of the gospel, expresses a wider hope (Rom. 5:18; 11:32; 1 Cor. 15:22; Eph. 1:10; 1 Tim. 2:4). The two sets of statements are not incompatible because they are different *types* of statement. Paul's are 'detached' theological statements, addressed to Christians, about the purpose of God. Jesus' are 'existential' statements, designed not to propound a theological theory but to goad his hearers to change the direction of their lives. Jesus was warning of the real danger that unless you repent you will come to total misery, 'but it does not follow from the fact of this danger that you or I or anyone else is in fact never going to repent and be saved.'[34]

Hick deals with the issue of human freedom with an argument from the doctrine of creation. God has made us for himself, with a 'bias' towards him. Since our nature, seeking its own fulfilment and good, leads us towards him, the notion that the salvation of all men is possible only by God's coercion is set aside. So it is not a matter of God working *against* human freedom. Rather we should think of him as a psychiatrist helping the patient – both before death and beyond – to remove inner blockages and inhibitions. Hick's universalism is thus integrated both into his approach to eschatology from the perspective of theodicy, and into his theory that life after death takes the form of a series of lives in which the self grows towards perfection and the vision of God.[35]

The limitations of universalism

All these expositions of universalism have something to commend them. They have a fine emphasis on God's love: indeed, he who has

---

[34] *Ibid.*, p. 250.

[35] It is integrated also into his understanding of the relationship between Christianity and other religions: Jesus is not an exclusive disclosure of God, demanding faith in him for salvation, but is one of many ways in which God has revealed himself through the various religions. See *God and the Universe of Faiths* (London, 1973), esp. pp. 133–147.

not felt deeply the attraction of universalism can scarcely have been moved by the greatness of God's love. And all of them grapple to some extent with the reality of sin and divine judgment. But I am not persuaded that any of them deals satisfactorily with the tension in the New Testament between divine love and human freedom. The following observations are relevant.

a. The universalist and his critic agree entirely that God's will is to draw all men to himself. But whereas the universalist claims that for all men *not* to be saved would be a defeat for God and is therefore unthinkable, the anti-universalist believes that God will go on respecting the freedom of those who resist him – even though it causes him the utmost anguish, and even though it means that his will is not fully realized. Hick invites us to picture God as a divine psychiatrist guiding men to their true goal. But what of the man who refuses to go to the psychiatrist? Hick underplays man's 'bias' *against* God.

b. Robinson's argument that God's love is bound in the end to break down all barriers, and Hick's argument that our human nature with its bias towards God, will in the end lead us towards God, both raise the same problem. Does our experience confirm the view that as time goes on men's resistance to the love of another – or of God – always breaks down? Is it not psychologically and spiritually true that persistent refusal to respond to love makes response harder rather than easier? The more often we are moved to do something and fail to do it, the less likely it is that we will ever do it.

c. A period of purgation after death, during which a person moves from rebellion or imperfect response towards a complete openness to God, is an essential part of the schemes of Paternoster, Perry and Hick. It is not clear where Moule and Robinson stand on this issue, but the view seems to be presupposed by their assertion that God's victory will be won in co-operation with men's freedom (since clearly some people do die in a state of open rebellion towards God). But this major part of the argument finds no support in the New Testament. Admittedly, as has often been pointed out, many of Jesus' exhortations to decision in view of the coming crisis refer to the crisis created by his own ministry rather than to the crisis of the individual's death. But it is equally true that there are no reported sayings of Jesus which suggest the idea of remedial punishment or the possibility of a person's destiny being reversed after death.[36] Hick picks up clues from one or two of Jesus' parables, *e.g.*, 'You will never get out till you have paid the last penny' (Mt. 5:26; *cf.* 18:34f.).[37] These suggest a finite penalty, rather than an eternal hell. But it is widely agreed now that the details of parables are an insecure foundation for Christian doctrine – and Hick himself would be unlikely to fasten on such details unless they happened to fit his theory. The idea of remedial punishment or of the steady transformation of persons after death is a guess which contradicts the general thrust of Scripture.

One of the reasons underlying Hick's belief that a process of transformation goes on after death is that he finds it difficult to believe that God perfects men instantaneously at death. For it is far from clear that a person so transformed would be 'in any morally significant sense the same person as the frail, erring mortal who had lived and died'.[38] And if that is true for the believer, it may be extended to include the view that the unbeliever also has opportunities to respond to God and be transformed after death. But Hick himself argues that the life to come must be different from this life, beyond our powers to imagine.[39] So he is not justified in claiming that a gradual purgation after death is necessary on the grounds that we in this life have no experience of instantaneous transformation into morally perfect beings. Moreover, we may argue that, since a moment of conversion is a moment of fundamental and radical change which does not destroy the continuity of the person, it is no more difficult in principle to believe that at the moment of death or resurrection there takes place a moral transformation which is total and yet does not destroy the continuity of the person. By contrast, the argument for gradual purgation undermines the doctrine of God's grace.

d. The challenge of non-Christian religions does not require us *either* to surrender the uniqueness of Christ as God's supreme revelation and means of salvation, *or* to consign all adherents of all non-Christian religions to hell. It is quite possible to develop a theology which holds that God's offer of salvation is focused in Christ and

---

[36] W. Strawson, *Jesus and the Future Life*, p. 149.
[37] *Death and Eternal Life*, p. 244.
[38] *Evil and the God of Love*, p. 347.   [39] *Ibid.*, p. 352.

made available through him; and that people who lived before Christ, or after Christ but in non-Christian cultures, may find salvation through him on account of their trusting response to what they know of God. It is for God himself to determine how much of himself is truly disclosed through any particular religion. And it is for us to remember that in any religious context, including a Christian one, 'saving faith' involves coming to the end of one's 'religion' and abandoning oneself to the grace of God.[40]

e. Both Hick and Robinson stress that the New Testament's exhortations to repentance and warnings of eternal condemnation are a different type of statement from the statements about God's universal plan of salvation. They are 'existential' statements, underlining the urgency of choice. But what is the use – or the morality – of an existential threat which turns out to have no corresponding reality? The attempts of both scholars to deal with this problem seem to me to fail completely to cope with the case of a man who refuses to heed the warnings.[41]

f. What, then, are we to say about New Testament texts which speak in universalist terms – passages such as Romans 11:32, 36; 1 Corinthians 15:24–28; Ephesians 1:9f.; Colossians 1:19f.? The first thing to say is that they have to be taken seriously, as traditional Christianity has usually not taken them seriously: they suggest a wider hope and a more enterprising and comprehensive approach to mission than most Christians have ever entertained. Yet such texts cannot justifiably be used as an argument for universal salvation.

In the first place, the idea of God being 'all in all' – which Robinson makes much of – does not self-evidently imply that all men will willingly surrender to God's purpose. It is a statement of God's universal sovereignty, but that authority would not be impaired by a two-fold outcome at the final judgment.[42]

Secondly, nearly all such 'universalist' statements occur alongside

[40] For a brief discussion of this issue, with evaluation of various viewpoints, see J. N. D. Anderson, 'A Christian Approach to Comparative Religion', in Anderson (ed.), *The World's Religions* (London, [4]1975), pp. 228–237.

[41] J. A. T. Robinson, *In the End God*, p. 129; J. Hick, *Death and Eternal Life*, p. 249.

[42] Cf. H. Schwarz, *On the Way to the Future* (Minneapolis, 1972), p. 148. A helpful discussion of the background and meaning of the phrase 'all in all' is in H. Conzelmann, *1 Corinthians* (ET, Philadelphia, 1975), p. 275. For a fuller discussion of 'universalist' biblical texts, see N. T. Wright, 'Towards a Biblical View of Universalism', *Themelios* 4.2, January 1979, pp. 54–58.

statements about the need for faith in order to experience salvation. In Colossians 1:19–23, for example, God's purpose of 'reconciling to himself all things' is said to include the Gentiles at Colossae, '*provided that* you continue in the faith. . . .' It seems preferable, therefore, to understand these 'universalist' statements not as statements of what *will* happen, but as declarations that God's saving *purpose* has universal scope, even though some people may refuse to enter into that purpose. But Paul consistently refused to dogmatize about the eternal destiny of any particular individual, and we would be wise to follow his example.

The nature of 'eternal punishment'

If it is true that not all men will find salvation, what will be the nature of the destiny of unbelievers? There are two alternative views, eternal punishment or annihilation (also known as conditional immortality).

The traditional view, that those who meet the last judgment unsuccessfully will suffer endless torment, is still maintained by some scholars. R. Gleason, apparently basing his argument on belief in the soul's immortality, says that 'the soul in hell is in an eternal vacuum of the emotions, violently existing in the face of one long thirst for love.' 'The psychological agony of hell is brought about because God allows the soul to realize the sinful tendencies it displayed on earth. . . . God has, so to speak, ratified the selfish will of the soul in hell.' We should not interpret hell as if it were a denial of the opportunity to repent his crime to a sinner who would do so. The sinner in hell is a rebel for ever.[43] Another Roman Catholic, J. Staudinger, quotes a series of biblical texts (including Mt. 25:34, 41, 46; Mk. 9:42f.; 2 Thes. 1:9; Rev. 14:11; 19:3; 20:10) and later ecclesiastical statements in support of the belief. And he argues that eternal punishment for a sinful act committed in a moment is justified because the sin of a moment causes results (*i.e.*, spiritual death) which man of his own power can never undo.[44]

The American Reformed theologian H. Buis claims that eternal punishment is the plain teaching of Scripture, though he criticizes

[43] *The World to Come*, pp. 118f., 126.
[44] *Life Hereafter* (ET, Dublin, 1964), pp. 210–214.

those who interpret images such as 'worm' and 'fire' too literally. There will be degrees of punishment – Hitler's fate is worse than that of the average decent unbelieving American. Thus the requirements of justice will be met. The annihilationist view is to be rejected because annihilation is not so much a punishment as an escape from punishment, and because words like 'destruction' and 'death' (which the annihilationist makes much of) imply in the Bible not extinction but the absence of life in relationship to God.[45]

H. Schwarz also opts for eternal punishment rather than annihilation, and observes that the New Testament pictures hell in terms of pain, despair and loneliness. 'These negative experiences express the reaction to the disclosure and finalization of the discrepancy between the eternal destiny of man and his realization of this destiny. They express the anguish of knowing what one has missed without the possibility of ever reaching it.'[46]

Immortality of the soul, divine justice, and the explicit teaching of Scripture are thus the main grounds of belief in eternal punishment.

Belief in the annihilation of the unbeliever at death or at the final judgment, so that he simply ceases to exist, began to gain ground in the mid-nineteenth century.[47] Arguments used to support this view include the following.

a. The Bible does not teach that the soul is naturally immortal, but that resurrection is a gift of God. This suggests that God grants resurrection to those who love him, but those who resist him go out of existence.[48]

b. Many biblical images suggest annihilation rather than continuing conscious existence. 'Fire' as an image of judgment suggests destruction. 'Death' indicates the end of all life, the condition of the person separated from God who is the source of life.[49]

[45] *The Doctrine of Eternal Punishment* (Philadelphia, 1957). *Cf.* L. Boettner, *Immortality* (London, 1956), pp. 117–123; W. Hendriksen, *The Bible on the Life Hereafter* (Grand Rapids, 1959), pp. 195–204.
[46] *On the Way to the Future*, pp. 222f.
[47] See Rowell, *Hell and the Victorians*, pp. 180–21 .
[48] See the discussion of resurrection and immortality above, pp. 95ff.
[49] *Cf.* M. Paternoster, *Thou Art There Also*, pp. 32f. Strawson argues that Jesus' use of 'Hades', 'Gehenna' and other images implies extinction rather than eternal punishment (*Jesus and the Future Life*, pp. 128–149). For a different understanding of death in the Bible see L. Morris, *The Wages of Sin* (London, 1954).

c. It is true that the fate of the lost is sometimes spoken of in the New Testament as 'eternal' punishment (notably in Mt. 25:46; *cf.* 2 Thes. 1:9; Heb. 6:2). But 'eternal' signifies the permanence of the *result* of judgment rather than the continuous operation of the act of punishment itself. So 'eternal punishment' means an act of judgment whose results are irreversible; it does not imply that the experience of being punished goes on for ever.

d. Eternal torment serves no useful purpose, and is therefore merely vindictive. This vindictiveness is incompatible with the love of God in Christ.[50]

e. Eternal torment involves an eternal cosmological dualism, which is impossible to reconcile with the conviction that ultimately God will be 'all in all'.

It is difficult to decide between annihilation and eternal torment on purely exegetical grounds. Terms like 'destruction' and 'Gehenna' are not precise enough for a clear-cut decision. And the New Testament writers deal largely in images rather than in precise theological definition. But certainly the biblical evidence for eternal punishment is considerably less than is popularly supposed. The seemingly uncreative vindictiveness of eternal punishment, together with the eternal cosmic dualism which it necessitates, might tip the scale in favour of annihilation.[51] Admittedly, these are philosophical rather than biblical arguments, and it may be objected that a doctrine plainly taught in Scripture is to be accepted as God's truth even if it does raise philosophical problems. However, the claim of the conditionalist is that the 'traditional orthodoxy' of eternal torment arose in the early church precisely because biblical teaching was (illegitimately) interpreted in the light of Platonic philosophy, which involved belief in the immortality of the soul and in everlasting punishment. Thus the argument about the status of philosophical considerations cuts both ways.

J. W. Wenham, in a careful and fuller discussion than has been possible here, makes two complementary suggestions. First, he argues that the traditional case for eternal torment should not lightly be surrendered. Secondly, he believes that the case for conditional immortality deserves to be considered much more seriously by con-

---

[50] *Cf.* J. Baillie, *And the Life Everlasting*,. pp. 240–244.
[51] See the brief survey in J. A. Baird, *The Justice of God in the Teaching of Jesus*, pp. 228–236.

servative thinkers than it has been hitherto. He cites two writers who certainly had no wish to evade the full teaching of Scripture – H. E. Guillebaud and B. F. C. Atkinson – who made out a strong case for conditionalism.[52] There is here an important issue for debate, a debate in which for half a century scholars have hardly engaged at all.

Nevertheless, a sense of proportion is required. The very ambiguity of the biblical evidence ought to suggest to us that this was an issue of secondary importance to the New Testament writers. We saw earlier that judgment and salvation are to be understood in terms of relationship to God. In keeping with this, the most significant thing about the destiny of unbelievers is that they will be separated from Christ. Compared with that tragic fact, there is – according to the New Testament writers – little point in asking whether the lost continue to be conscious or are annihilated. It is because later Christians have been more concerned about happiness and misery than about relationship to God that they have persisted in asking such questions.

Finally, it should be stressed that, while the New Testament clearly teaches the seriousness of judgment based on our moral choices, it does not encourage us to make the fate of any particular individual into a dogmatic issue. As Strawson says, 'The most important question of all is not, What can I think about eternal life?, but What must I do to inherit eternal life?' And on Jesus' refusal to predict the number of those who would be saved (Lk. 13:23f.), he comments: 'Jesus . . . places no limit upon the number of the saved, except men's willingness or unwillingness to accept the conditions.'[53]

---

[52] J. W. Wenham *The Goodness of God* (London, 1974), pp. 27–41, citing H. E. Guillebaud, *The Righteous Judge* (1964), and B. F. C. Atkinson, *Life and Immortality* (no date). He notes that both these books were published privately, since suspicion of heresy apparently made it difficult for the authors to get their works accepted by publishers. The most comprehensive defence of conditionalism is by the Seventh-Day Adventist L. E. Froom, *The Conditionalist Faith of Our Fathers*, 2 volumes (Washington DC, 1965, 1966).

[53] *Jesus and the Future Life*, p. 229.

Afterword

There have been books with titles like *Last Things First* and *The Last Things Now* – titles suggesting that eschatology is not a remote topic about remote events, fit only for consignment to a brief appendix in systematic theologies, but that eschatology concerns men's lives *now* and Christ's relationship to *now*.[1] This is a welcome and essential emphasis. Yet one of the contentions of this book has been that whatever the relevance of eschatology for the present, eschatology is about 'the last things'. Indeed, its relevance for the present derives from its concern with 'the last things'. Without a genuinely future consummation of God's purpose for the world and for individuals, his purpose in the present becomes pointless. Thus it has been argued:

a. that apocalyptic, with its belief in resurrection and its cosmic scope, has an important contribution to make to Christian thought;

b. that the parousia as a future event is an integral part of salvation history;

c. that a Christianity without a personal, fulfilled and yet corporate life after death is a contradiction in terms. As Josef Pieper puts it: 'How can there be any talk of hope when the thing hoped for is so conceived that the being who is alone capable of hoping, namely the individual person, cannot have it?'[2]

d. that the reality of a future divine judgment is important for a fully human life now, since responsibility is an essential aspect of being human;

e. that these various themes find their proper relationship to each other in their being related to Jesus Christ and his work.

But whilst it seems to me important to stress these things, it is

[1] E. G. Rupp, *Last Things First* (London, 1964); D. L. Edwards, *The Last Things Now* (London, 1969).

[2] *Hope and History* (ET, London, 1969), p. 71.

equally important to resist the temptation to assert too much. There are those who claim the ability to devise timetables of the future as though they had already been there. But this is to ignore the pictorial nature of at least some eschatological language, and to ignore the ambiguities in Scripture over such matters as the relationship between resurrection and judgment. It also normally involves assuming, rather than justifying, a particularly literalistic method of interpreting the Bible.

There remain matters over which definite opinions are difficult or impossible, because of the complexities of the biblical evidence or the inherent difficulties of the subject. Eschatological hope is in any case not capable of empirical demonstration, but is essentially a matter of extrapolation from present experience of God, and of trustful acceptance of what the God thus experienced, is believed to have revealed through Christ and his apostles.

There are matters, too, which might have found their way into a book such as this but have not done so. In particular, there is the vital matter of the implications of eschatology for present experience and action in the world. Fortunately, the Christian does not have to choose between his personal immortality and a hope for men's future in the world. Indeed, now that 'theology of hope' and 'political theology' and 'liberation theology' have had some years of attention by theologians, a major task is the creation of a synthesis between these 'worldly hopes' and a theology of human immortality in fellowship with God.

Only where these two aspects of hope are held in tension can genuine Christian hope be said to exist, and only then can the future of man be said to be rightly understood. For a hope that is merely other-worldly fails to do justice to the fact that 'the God of hope' (*cf.* Rom. 15:13) is the Creator of this world and has taken action in it: the kingdom of God has been inaugurated in Jesus Christ. But the hope that is only for this world makes a mockery of all those who in past generations have hoped and worked for the transformation of this world but have failed to see it; and such a hope, being transient, is unworthy of the God revealed in Christ and in his resurrection. What is more, the Christian concept of heaven as a sphere of love, community and justice indicates what goals and values should be the objects of hope and action. And the Holy

Spirit, understood by Paul as 'the first fruits' (Rom. 8:23) and 'the guarantee of our inheritance' (2 Cor. 1:22; Eph. 1:14) provides the enabling and sustaining power for Christian hope and action.[3]

There is room, then, for differences of opinion, room for reverent agnosticism, but also for worship, action and hope in the light of 'what no eye has seen, nor ear heard, nor the heart of man conceived, what God has prepared for those who love him' (1 Cor. 2:9).

---

[3] I have tried in a popular way to show what practical implications Christian eschatology might have for spirituality and for personal and social ethics, in *The Jesus Hope* (Hemel Hempstead, 1974) and again in *I Believe in the Second Coming of Jesus Christ* (London, forthcoming). See also (among others) R. Aldwinckle, *Death in the Secular City* (London, 1972), pp. 172–184; J. Ellul, *Hope in Time of Abandonment* (New York, 1973). D. F. Wells has discussed political theology in *The Search for Salvation* (Leicester, 1978), pp. 119–139; and J. A. Kirk has discussed liberation theology in *Theology Encounters Revolution* (Leicester, 1980) and *Liberation Theology* (London, 1979).

Index